D1284213

The
Egg White
Cookbook

The Egg White Cookbook

RECIPES FOR EVERY MEAL,
FEATURING NATURE'S
PERFECT PROTEIN

Margaret Blackstone
& Barbara Leopold

M. Evans and Company, Inc.
New York

Copyright © 2005 by Margaret Blackstone and Barbara Leopold

All rights reserved. No part of this book may be reproduced or transmitted in any form or by any means, electronic or mechanical, including photocopying, recording, or by any information storage and retrieval system, without prior permission in writing from the publisher.

M. Evans and Company, Inc.
216 East 49th Street
New York, NY 10017

Library of Congress Cataloging-in-Publication Data

Blackstone, Margaret.
 The egg white cookbook : recipes for every meal, featuring nature's
perfect protein / Margaret Blackstone and Barbara Leopold.
  p. cm.
 ISBN 1-59077-071-4
 1. Cookery (Eggs) I. Leopold, Barbara. II. Title.
 TX745.B62 2005
 641.6'75--dc22
         2005008481

Designed by Evan Johnston and Chrissy Kwasnik

Printed in the United States of America

9 8 7 6 5 4 3 2 1

Dedication

In memory of my father, Henry Blackstone
and to my son, Dashiell Henry Lunde
M.B.

To my family, Tom, Olivia, and Augusta
who inspire me to try new things every day.
B.L.

Heaven is like an egg, and the earth is like the yolk of the egg.
—CHANG HENG

Clearly, then, the egg white is heaven.
—THE AUTHORS

CONTENTS

ACKNOWLEDGEMENTS

Firstly, we would like to thank each other for ham and egg whiting it through thick and thin.

Thanks also go to Dr. Shari Butler who first touted egg white omelets to us as comfort food. We also thank our friends Joyce Engelson, Jean Dunkirk, and Anna McCormick for contributing their recipes. And, of course, thanks to our families, friends, and knitting buddies for tasting so many of our recipes more than once and to our dogs, Lily and Henry, for helping us by eating the yolks.

Finally, we would like to thank our agent, Gene Brissie, our editor PJ Dempsey, and all of the staff at M. Evans for their dedication to the project and their help on the book.

INTRODUCTION

The Egg White Way

*Put all your eggs in one basket
and watch that basket.*
—Mark Twain

One Saturday morning we visited the wonderful farmer's market in New York City's Union Square and found ourselves at an organic meat and poultry stand. Next to us stood a stylish, healthy-looking, older couple. While we pondered the organic chickens, the elegant woman suddenly captured our attention. She had just ordered four dozen organic eggs. We found ourselves a little stunned. How, we wondered, could two people reach such an age looking so well while eating that many eggs. "Excuse me," Meg said, trying not to sound too nosy. "So many eggs? Is that so healthy for the two of you?"

The woman laughed and took her husband's arm, smiling wisely, "Oh, we toss the yolks. We only use the whites." She then went on to tell us more. She was in the habit of hard-boiling the eggs, tossing the yolks, and making batches of egg white salad, using some chopped celery, capers, scallions, and low-fat mayonnaise. She and her husband dined on egg white salads or egg white salad sandwiches for lunch and sometimes even had egg white salad for breakfast. Well, you get the idea. A chance encounter on a beautiful spring day ended up elevating egg whites far above the level of a breakfast substitute for us. Life in our kitchens was about to change.

Soon after that Saturday morning outing, the idea for *The Egg White Cookbook* was born. Friends for years, we have cooked together and our families have shared many a meal. Meg was more author than chef, and Barbara was more chef than author. We decided we would make a good team and began to collaborate on the book and the recipes for the book.

We had always marveled at the egg white's magical properties in cooking, from its ability to bind oil and vinegar to form a silken vinaigrette to the wondrous transformation that takes place when whipping liquid egg whites to snowy, feathery peaks, as in a meringue. We looked forward to using these versatile egg whites to create tasty, healthy, and even economical meals. By this time in American culinary evolution, everybody knows about egg white omelets, but how about egg whites in the rest of the day's meals—lunch, dinner, and dessert, and what about delicious egg white snacks and appetizers? This became our challenge.

We settled on approximately seventy-five recipes and got to work. We found ourselves enjoying almost every minute of the job and eating our way through a delicious new world, a testament to friendship and our interest in our new favorite food. As the recipes began to take shape, we took the show on the road, testing dinner recipes on our families and creating a series of egg white luncheons, including one in which we actually convinced our literary agent to let us give him an egg white and oatmeal facial before eating lunch. (Henry, Barbara's Boston Terrier, nearly ate the facial before it could even be applied.) Our agent enjoyed his rejuvenating facial and then went on to devour the delicious luncheon of White Hearts Salad sandwiches, Egg White Caesar Salad, and Chocolate-Chocolate Chip Angel Food Cake for dessert. And so we were on our way.

What we now refer to as the Chai Tea Pudding incident began innocently enough when we were inspired while sipping some Chai Tea Latte. We decided to combine the great flavors of that drink into a dessert pudding. The pudding was wonderful (you'll find it in the dessert section), except for one thing: we neglected to take into account that the tea is loaded with caffeine. When Barbara tested the pudding on her family, she was delighted by their rave reviews, but she was not so delighted when the caffeine in the pudding kept the family up all night. Unless you are a night owl, we recommend using decaffeinated tea bags in the pudding. Aside from this one nearly sleepless night, we have found our egg white adventure to be inspiring, healthy, delicious, and ongoing in the pleasures it brings to us and our families and friends.

Our recipe repertoires have expanded and our cooking skills have been honed by such extended concentration—all thanks to the lovely lady at the farmer's market and her egg white wisdom.

If you doubt the viability of the egg white as the centerpiece for dinner recipes, we hope the recipes in this book will convince you otherwise. We've

found egg whites to be versatile enough to use in everything from Greek Salt-Crusted Halibut (page 118) to Pasta Carbonara and Chili, including expanding the uses of egg whites far beyond egg whites breakfasts and desserts.

When Meg's son, Dash, was about to go on a class trip to Spain, sponsored by his school in honor of eighth-grade graduation, we threw a send-off party for him and served Black and White Chili (recipe on page 110). It certainly was a crowd-pleaser. The chili is a great dish for a crowd because it can be made days ahead, except for the egg whites, which can be cooked and added as the dish is heated just before serving. By the way, Dash had thirds.

If you really find yourself going "eggy" over egg whites, you may also want to begin to experiment with eggs from other fowl, as we did when we visited the home of an animal rescuer on Long Island. Her house was a cross between a veterinarian's practice and a small farm. She had rescued bunnies, dogs and cats, a goat or two, and a great number of hens. One happened to lay eggs with the most beautiful, pale, opalescent, green shells, reminiscent of the first new green leaves of spring. This chicken was one of a Peruvian variety named the Araucana. Little did our kind-hearted animal lover know what an exotic waif she had rescued, but how lucky she was.

She gave each of us a half dozen eggs to take home with us, enabling both of our families to enjoy the most delicious Cheesy Whites (see page 27) we'd ever tasted and inspiring a host of jokes about green eggs and ham (only the shells of the eggs are green). Because the whites of these eggs are particularly tasty, we prefer them for scrambling and in our White Hearts Salad (page 82).

Eggs are not only for eating. As we began to cook and talk about egg whites more and more, we came up with other interesting uses for this versatile protein. We began to explore other creative ways to use the whites and to deal with those left-over yolks. We found that the whites may be healthier for eating, but the yolks have benefits of their own for non-food uses. For example, we created both egg white and egg yolk facials. Egg white facials work best on oily skin. The yolk facials moisturize dry skin. We even went so far as to create eggshell ornaments, tips for using eggshells in the garden soil, and how to use the shells to prevent bitter-tasting coffee. We tried to think of everything involving all parts of the egg. You'll find the non-food recipes in the final section of the book.

There was something about the creative challenge of coming up with a variety of flavorful dishes created around the egg white that began to inspire healthier eating all the way around. We were also pleasantly surprised at what a

relief it was not to have the sulfurous smell of the egg yolks in our kitchens.

To say the least, in our households "egg" has become synonymous with egg white. For example, one morning Meg was scrambling egg whites with an organic rice cheese substitute, when her son requested, "Mom, may I please have some of your eggs?" If we have succeeded in doing what we set out to do in writing this book, you and your family will begin to think in the same way.

Chapter 1
All About
Egg Whites

Yes! You can make an omelet without breaking eggs. All you have to do is use liquid egg white products.
—The Authors

The egg white albumen is the unsung protein hero in the current diet wars. Because of the great nutritional value of egg whites and the low caloric content, many current diet plans are recommending egg whites as a major protein source. Therefore, it is great to discover just how versatile egg whites are. In fact, egg whites can shine as the centerpiece of any meal of the day, provide the protein you need, and fill you up so that you don't overeat.

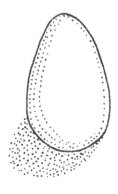

Nature's Perfect Protein

Egg protein is commonly referred to as the perfect protein because it scores a 1.0, the highest measure, on the protein digestibility corrective amino acid score, meaning that anyone, including the elderly and those who might suffer from digestive problems, would benefit from making egg whites a major protein source in their diet. It also scores 100 on the biological value, meaning all ingested protein is retained or reused by the body.

Egg protein has long been a staple of body-building nutrition. In fact, it should be noted that "Egg White Poppers," are hard-cooked egg white cubes that body builders pop into their mouths when they need a protein boost.

THE ANATOMY OF AN EGG WHITE

There are many interesting facts about albumen egg whites, for instance:

- The fat component of the egg white is good fat, mono- and polyunsaturated, while the fat contained in the yolk is mostly saturated fat.

- Egg whites contain no cholesterol.

- Most of the protein in an egg is in the egg white (see the following chart).

- Egg whites are a perfect choice for vegetarians as an economical and complete protein alternative.

- Albumen is easier to digest than the protein found in meat, fish, and poultry.

- The protein content of an egg white meal goes to work immediately and causes less stress to your digestive system.

- The composition of the egg white is seven-eighths water, making for an extremely low caloric value.

- Egg white contains choline, an essential nutrient for brain development and memory.
- The USDA Center for Nutrition's Food Pyramid suggests that you add more egg whites to your diet, precisely because they have no cholesterol and no saturated fat.

THE NUTRITIONAL VALUE OF AN EGG			
Part	*Calories*	*Protein*	*Fat*
Egg White	16	3.5 grams	minimal, if any (mono- and polyunsaturated fat only)
Egg Yolk	59	2 grams	5 grams (saturated fat)

Most of us who use eggs in cooking take them for granted. We know what we need to know about eggs and think that is about all there is to know, but when eggs become the central focus of a dish, it is important to get to know all you can about eggs.

TESTING FOR FRESHNESS

The freshness, type, and taste of the egg take center stage when cooking with just the whites. Therefore, it is important to pay particular attention to the freshness of eggs when using the recipes in this cookbook because the freshest eggs have a far superior eggy taste in our opinion.

The freshness of eggs is apparent in their appearance. As an egg ages, the whites become thinner and the yolks flatter, but this does not compromise their nutritional value or their functional cooking properties. Consumers can easily tell the age of an egg as egg cartons from USDA-inspected egg-packing plants must display the date the eggs were packed along with an expiration date, which is usually thirty days beyond the packing date.

Shell eggs can be tested for freshness if you don't know when they were packed by checking the appearance of the uncooked whites. A raw egg white will appear very cloudy when it is very fresh due to the presence of carbon dioxide, less so if it is a few weeks old. Another way to test for freshness is to submerge the egg in a bowl of water. The higher it floats, the older it is. Really fresh eggs will sink. Though it happens rarely, eggs can eventually spoil. Spoiled eggs have a sour or fruity odor and are blue-green in color. Of course, they should not be eaten. When using the egg white products sold in containers at your local market, be sure to check the dates on the packaging and follow the instructions for handling and storing.

STORING EGGS

According to the American Egg Board, eggs are safe to eat four to five weeks beyond the packing date if they are properly stored in their cartons (large end up to keep the air cell in place) and kept refrigerated in the lower (colder) shelves (not the door shelf provided for individual egg storage) below forty degrees.

Government regulations require that eggs be carefully washed and sanitized before packing. The hens' original, protective egg coating is generally replaced by a thin coating of mineral oil, so don't wash your store-bought eggs, as you will remove this protective coating. The egg shell has thousands of tiny pores on its surface, so eggs should be stored in their cartons to prevent them from picking up odors from other foods in the refrigerator. Eggs age more in one day at room temperature than from one week in the refrigerator. Discard any eggs with unclean, cracked, or leaking shells.

Candling

Candling is the process that egg-packaging plants use to detect cracked shells and interior defects of the eggs. During candling, eggs travel along a conveyor belt and pass over a light source where the defects become visible. All eggs with defects are then discarded. It's called candling because this technique began before the advent of electricity when farmers only had candles for light.

GRADING THE EGG

The USDA provides a grading service in many egg-packing plants based on the interior and exterior qualities of the egg and designate it by the letters AA, A, and B in descending order of quality. There is no nutritive value difference between the grades. Most shell eggs and egg white products sold in supermarkets use AA or A grades eggs. It is very difficult to discern a taste distinction between the various grades.

EGG WHITE INFORMATION AND TECHNIQUES

Since for most of us eggs are simply what we eat or don't eat for breakfast, and egg whites are used in meringues, the following is a primer of the best techniques for cracking, separating, whipping, storing, and cooking egg whites, yolks, and commercially packaged egg white products.

Cracking and Separating Eggs

To prevent any bacteria that may be present on the outside of the shell from contaminating the egg's contents, you will need an inexpensive egg separator and two small bowls. Begin by taking a cold, clean egg and rapping it at its midsection on the edge of one of the bowls. Separate the shell halves and pour the contents through the egg separator that you have placed in one of the bowls. Wait until the egg white drips through the separator and the yolk remains in the cup-like center. Pour the yolk into the other bowl and repeat the process for the next egg.

Should you find yourself without an egg separator, you can always do it the old-fashioned way—by hand, literally. Start by washing and drying your hands. Then simply pour the cracked egg into your hand and let the white slip between your fingers into the bowl below with the yolk remaining in the palm of your hand. Another method is to crack open an egg and pour the cracked egg contents back and forth between the two halves of the broken shell until all the white has slipped into the bowl below. Using this method increases the risk of breaking the yolk and there is a chance of bacterial contamination from the broken shell itself.

Keep in mind that if you are separating egg whites with the intention of whipping them, they must be totally free of any yolk. If a bit of yolk does drip into the white, use a clean teaspoon to remove it.

Whipping Egg Whites

Room temperature eggs work best when whipping egg whites, so after separating cold eggs, you need to wait about 20 minutes until they reach room temperature before you begin to whip them (see Cracking and Separating Eggs). Both fresh egg whites and powdered whites work well for whipping, but pasteurized, commercially packaged liquid egg whites do not.

When whipping eggs, make sure to place the whites in a clean, grease-free bowl. It's a good idea to rinse the bowl with a little white vinegar to ensure that it's grease-free, and then dry it thoroughly.

A hand mixer is great at this task, although it is entirely possible to whip the whites by hand, preferably using a copper bowl especially reserved for this purpose, and it's good exercise to boot. Add a pinch of salt and the amount of cream of tartar recommended. Cream of tartar stabilizes beaten eggs so that they maintain their volume of air. Some recipes may call for lemon juice, which can also be used to stabilize the beaten whites.

Cleaning Up Raw Eggs

If you drop an egg, miss the bowl, or spill raw eggs on the floor or counter, sprinkle plenty of salt over the liquid, wait a minute, and then mop up. The salt will absorb much of the goopiness.

To begin the whipping process, start your mixer on a low speed, mix until the egg whites turn foamy and continue whipping until soft peaks form. If you are making a meringue, add the sugar slowly, one to two tablespoons at this time. Sugar also serves to increase the stability of the foam. Be sure to get your hand mixer down to the bottom of the bowl. You don't want to leave any liquid whites that have not been whipped. Then continue whipping until stiff peaks form. This can take anywhere from three to five minutes. Be careful not to over-beat your whites. They will look dry and start to break down when over-whipped.

If you're using dried whites and meringue powders, follow the manufacturer's directions on the label.

The Care and Feeding of a Copper (Egg) Whipping Bowl

You don't really need a copper bowl for the recipes in this book, but if you do have one, this is how to care for it. First, just use this bowl for eggs and nothing else and never let the eggs sit in the bowl a long time as they will turn green as they react with the copper.

Every time you use it, clean it with a paste of white vinegar and salt and rinse it well with water, before and after use, to remove any fat particles that will prevent egg whites from whipping. In cooking school, we learned to whip egg whites by hand, and the final test was turning the bowl over our heads to prove the egg whites were whipped thoroughly. Although egg whites are good for your hair, we were quite glad when the egg whites held, as we prefer to condition our hair at home.

Hard-Cooked Eggs

To hard-cook eggs perfectly, place raw, cold eggs in a saucepan. The size of the saucepan will vary depending on the number of eggs you are hard-cooking. Then cover with cold water, bring to boil over medium heat, and turn off the heat immediately. Do not allow eggs to boil. If the eggs are cooked too quickly, they will become tough and develop a green tinge around the yolk. Cover the saucepan and let sit for twelve minutes. Drain the hot water and run cold water over the eggs; let eggs sit ten minutes more. To peel, roll eggs to crack the shell and lift it off. Refrigerate hard-cooked eggs promptly and use within one week. Cooked yolks keep four to five days in a tightly sealed container. Cooked egg yolks can be stored in your freezer for up to one year as well when kept tightly wrapped until needed and defrosted in the refrigerator. Choose older eggs for hard-cooking as fresh eggs are harder to peel.

We do not recommend egg cookers. They add unnecessary clutter to the kitchen and a saucepan is the better choice because you can control the cooking process.

To tell if an egg is raw or hard-cooked, try spinning it on a flat surface. If it spins easily, it is hard-cooked.

Storing Raw Egg Whites and Yolks

If you are like us and hate to waste food, you'll be happy to know that raw egg whites and yolks store well in the refrigerator and the freezer. You can refrigerate raw whites for up to four days covered tightly in a clean container. Raw, unbroken yolks keep two days in a tightly sealed container.

Raw egg whites freeze beautifully, except if they are pasteurized shell eggs. Do not freeze these.

WHITES. Pour egg whites into an ice cube tray, one in each section, then cover the tray with plastic wrap, and freeze until they harden. Remove them from the tray and place in a plastic freezer bag labeled with the date. Frozen whites can be used for up to one year. To use, defrost the number of whites you need in a covered bowl in the refrigerator.

YOLKS. Raw egg yolks do not fare as well as whites when frozen, due to their gelatinous properties. However, adding small amounts of salt or sugar before freezing will keep the eggs viable for use. If you want to save the yolks for a dessert recipe, simply mix one and a half teaspoons of sugar with four large yolks before freezing. If you want to use the yolks later in a main dish, mix in an eighth of a teaspoon of salt with four large yolks before freezing. This significantly cuts down on the pasty texture common to frozen yolks. Keep the frozen yolks tightly wrapped and labeled with the date and use within one year. Defrost in the refrigerator.

PASTUERIZED SHELL EGGS

Pasteurized shell eggs are heat-treated, that is, brought to 140 degrees and held at that temperature for three and a half minutes to destroy bacteria. They are sold in some specialty markets and are especially useful in recipes like salad dressings or sauces where the egg white is not cooked per se. Pasteurized shell eggs are not recommended for whipping or freezing.

COOKING WITH EGG WHITES

It is best to cook egg whites slowly over gentle heat, especially for dishes like scrambled or poached eggs, omelets, and frittatas. This ensures the best taste and texture.

All cooked egg white dishes need to be cooked to an internal temperature of 160 degrees, according to government food safety guidelines. This means that when cooking scrambled eggs and omelets, the dish is done when no visible liquid egg remains. Hard-cooked egg whites easily reach an internal temperature of 160 degrees when done. If you're not sure, use a food thermometer inserted into the cooked food to check the internal temperature. Always serve egg dishes promptly after cooking or refrigerate.

BROWN, WHITE, OR GREEN

Europe has had domesticated hens since 600 B.C., and Christopher Columbus is said to have brought chickens to the New World on his second voyage across the Atlantic in 1493. So for over 500 years, chickens have been laying eggs on our shores and people have been consuming them.

The color of the egg shell depends on the breed of hen and does not affect the flavor or texture of the egg inside. Breeds with white feathers and white ear lobes lay white eggs. Breeds with red feathers and red ear lobes lay brown eggs. Since all brown egg layers, such as the Rhode Island Red, New Hampshire, and Plymouth Rock breeds, lay bigger eggs, brown eggs are usually more expensive. White eggs are the most common egg sold and come from a hardy reliable American hen. The beautiful, pastel-green eggs from a relatively rare breed, the Araucana, cost more due to their rarity, but we think their flavor is superior. If you have the chance to sample some of these eggs from a small, local producer or farm do not hesitate to do so.

ORGANIC AND FREE-RANGE EGGS

While many people are choosing to eat organic foods more and more, the debate still goes on over whether organic or natural foods are truly better, safer, or more nutritious to eat. You might see egg cartons in your local supermarket with labels such as "organic," "free range," or "natural." The USDA cautions against these labels, since they can be misleading.

With that in mind, however, we have found an organic brand of eggs in the process of testing our recipes that we have come to rely on for their really fresh taste and good quality. The producers, Pete and Gerry's Organic Eggs, sell their eggs over the internet (http://peteandgerrys/com). Their hens are "cage free," run free when possible, and lay their eggs in nests. They show good evidence of this on their web site. While the nutritional value of such eggs is not superior to that of other shell eggs, we found we loved the taste of these egg whites and use them when the egg white takes center stage in a recipe, such as Cheesy Whites or Smoked Turkey Hash with Poached Whites. (See the product information at the end of this section.)

SIZE MATTERS

Most commercial grade eggs are packaged according to size. The size of the egg or egg white matters when taking recipe proportions into account. For purposes of the recipes in this book, we use large eggs/whites, the most readily available in supermarkets. For the recipes in this book, use this conversion chart:

CONVERSION CHART
1 large egg white = 2 tablespoons liquid egg white product
1 large egg white = 2 teaspoons egg white powder + 2 tablespoons water

THE EGG WHITE PRODUCTS

There are numerous egg white products on the market today. They can be found in most supermarkets in the dairy section or, in the case of powdered whites, in the baking section. In creating and testing the recipes for this book, we had occasion to sample all of the most popular and readily available brands and have compiled a guide for you.

Liquid egg whites are pasteurized liquid egg whites sold in re-sealable cartons or in single-serving yogurt style containers in the refrigerated dairy case at the supermarket. Some commercial egg substitutes contain added vegetable oil, cellulous gums, beta carotene, non-fat milk, salt, and emulsifiers added for texture and color. They are fresh-tasting, have a pleasant egg-like texture when cooked, and are easy to store. They can be frozen in their containers for several weeks. They have a shelf life of ninety days after they leave the packaging plant and, after opening, the package can be kept in the refrigerator for seven days. They eliminate the need to separate the yolk and white. Another obvious advantage is that there is no waste (no yolk to discard) when using these products for egg white-only recipes. They can also be consumed uncooked safely because they are pasteurized. The best uses for these products is in shakes, omelets, batters, salad dressings, pasta dishes, meat dishes, coating for frying or baking and puddings and pies. Most liquid egg whites are very difficult to whip to stiff peaks so they are not suitable for meringues, soufflés, or angel food cakes. There are some brands which contain whipping agents (safe and suitable substances added as per FDA), which aid in the whipping process, such as Whippin' Whites.

A Brief Guide to Brands

- All Whites contains pure egg white, nothing added, and are sold in most supermarkets. Their Whippin' Whites contain the all-important whipping agents.

- Egg Beaters contains pure egg white, gums, and beta carotene to mimic the yolk color, except Egg Beaters All Whites, which do not contain any coloring. There are varieties of Egg Beaters that contain chopped vegetables, seasonings, and cheese. These can be found in most supermarkets.

- Eggology contains pure organic egg white, nothing added, and are kosher. These are sold in specialty markets, but more and more often can be found in general supermarkets.

- Lana's Egg Whites contains pure egg white, nothing added. These are sold over the internet at Lana's web site (http://www.lanaseggwhites.com).

MAKING A HOMEMADE EGG SUBSTITUTE

If you're looking for a product that has the yellow color of a whole egg, you can make your own egg substitute. Crack and separate three eggs and discard yolks. Add a pinch or two of egg shade paste for color and stir into the egg white. Use this in a recipe to replace two large eggs.

Egg shade is a tasteless food coloring used to mimic the egg yolk color. and can be found on the internet at http://www.barryfarm.com.

POWDERED EGG WHITES

Powdered egg whites have been used commercially for years but have recently shown up in supermarkets. Powdered egg whites are 100 percent dried albumen. They are sold in resealable cartons and can be found near the baking section of the supermarket. One obvious advantage is their long, twelve-month shelf life. They do not need refrigeration, even after opening. They are reconstituted by adding water to the powder. They whip like fresh egg whites and, because they are pasteurized, can be used safely without cooking or baking. They are also economical: a one-pound can is the equivalent of almost five dozen fresh eggs. Since they do not have the freshest taste, they are best used in meringues, icings, angel food cakes, cookies, or other recipes that call for lots of added seasoning or sugar.

The following are our favorite brands of powdered egg whites: Deb El, Just Whites, and Wilton Meringue Powder.

OIL AND MARGARINE PRODUCTS

For those of you who are concerned about fat content and the healthy application of this book, let us assure you that we use a good-quality cooking spray, canola oil, or olive oil for the recipes in this book. If you miss the taste of butter in a simple dish of scrambled egg whites, for example, you could certainly substitute a canola oil-based margarine. We recommend the following products, and, of course, it's up to you:

- Any brand of olive oil or canola oil cooking spray. You can make your own cooking spray by buying the oils in the bottle and transferring them to a spray bottle made for this purpose.

- Canola oil-based margarine. We use Canoleo Soft Margarine. It is made from 100-percent canola oil. It is an all-purpose margarine great for spreading, cooking, sautéing, and baking. It is an all-natural product and contains no preservatives. It has 50-percent less saturated fat than soy, safflower, or sunflower oil margarines. It is lactose-free and kosher.

- There are other brands of organic margarines on the market you may want to experiment with, and then, of course, there is always butter, though we don't use it in any of the recipes.

WHAT YOU WILL NEED
IN THE KITCHEN

For us, less is more when it comes to cooking gadgets that can quickly clutter up a kitchen, take up valuable counter space, and confuse the cook. We get by with minimal but good-quality cooking equipment. With that in mind, here are some basics, which we used again and again in creating the recipes for this book.

- **Nonstick skillets.** You will want to have at least three sizes of silicone-coated nonstick, heavy-bottomed skillets: a six-inch for a single egg white serving or small pancake, a nine- or ten-inch for omelets that serve four to six- and a twelve-inch for frittatas that serve eight to ten.

- **Egg poacher.** An electric or stovetop egg poacher, or an insert that fits inside a regular skillet, makes the tasks of poaching egg whites simple, although you can poach egg whites without one (see recipe on page 26).

- **George Foreman Countertop Electric Grill.** This is one of the best kitchen appliances ever invented. If you don't already have one, consider getting one and you'll not know how you ever lived without it. You will find yourself using it again and again in preparing sandwiches, French toast, vegetables, meat, fish, and just about anything, without having to add any fat.

- **Oven thermometer.** Even the fanciest oven needs one of these inexpensive gadgets to monitor the exact oven temperature as all ovens are calibrated differently. Place it in the middle of the oven on a rack and preheat your oven for at least fifteen minutes. Read the temperature as soon as you open the oven door and compare it with the oven temperature to which you have set your oven. You might have to adjust the temperature or cooking time accordingly.

- **Electric hand mixer.** There is no better or quicker way to whip egg whites than with this tool. Any hand mixer will do; no need to invest in an expensive standing mixer for any of the recipes in this book.

- **Egg separator.** This inexpensive and handy stainless steel gadget is really helpful when separating whites from yolks.

- **Wand blender.** This nifty little blender is another great kitchen invention because you can stick it directly into a pot or skillet to purée a hot soup without fear of being burned. Less cleanup and less mess means it's a useful gadget.

- **Wire and plastic whisks.** Keep several sizes handy: a balloon whisk to whip egg whites by hand; a small, thinner whisk for mixing egg whites in batters; and a tiny wire or plastic whisk for whisking whites for single omelets or scrambled dishes.

- **Rubber spatulas.** Invest in the new brightly colored silicone ones. They perform double duty since they're heat resistant, allowing you to use them directly in the pot or pan to stir or cook hot foods, scramble egg whites, or flip omelets.

- **Silicone glove and pot holders and nonstick Silpat (silicone) baking liners.** These recent inventions will make life and clean up in the kitchen a lot easier. They are heat-resistant, waterproof, washable, and virtually indestructible. The gloves have built-in grippers to help you grip hot food. The pot holders are attractive and durable enough to double as trivets. The baking liners, though they seem expensive at first glance, are nonstick, reusable, and never have to replaced.

Knives

We recommend that you buy good-quality knives and keep them sharpened. To keep it simple, you might want to start with the following and then add more to your collection as you find it necessary.

- One or two paring knives. A three-inch blade, stainless steel and heavy for its size, will get the most use in your kitchen.
- A chef's (or chopping) knife, a seven- to nine-inch stainless steel blade, heavy for its size, will also get a lot of use over time. Find one that fits comfortably in your hand; with proper care and maintenance, this knife should last a long time.
- A serrated slicing knife. A ten-inch stainless steel blade will be used endlessly for slicing breads, cakes, vegetables, and meats. It is difficult to sharpen this once it gets dull, so it will have to be replaced from time to time.

Keeping Your Knives Sharp

A sharp knife prevents accidents when you are preparing food because you don't need to exert as much pressure to cut through food, making slippage less likely to happen. You can sharpen your own knives with a good-quality knife sharpener such as a Chantry knife sharpener.

For high-quality, expensive knives, we recommend that you have them professionally sharpened once a year. Store your knives on a magnetized rack over the kitchen counter for easy and safe access.

WHAT WE LEARNED

On our journey down the egg white path, we discovered some important benefits:

- We cooked healthier, low-fat, low cholesterol dishes.
- We lost weight without trying, not to mention keeping our cholesterol levels in check.
- Cooking with egg whites is an excellent way to combine comfort foods with healthy foods.
- You can't beat Mother Nature's gift of a perfectly packaged protein. Cooking with egg whites is satisfying, convenient, quick, and versatile.

We hope our book will help you to experiment as you learn to create more than just omelets for breakfast. We wanted to share with you how to cook delicious lunches, appetizers, dinner entrées, and desserts that will satisfy and fill you up (before you eat too much). These recipes are so tasty that you may find, like us, that you are eating egg whites at various meals more than a few times a week.

There is more to the egg white than meets the eye. As one of nature's most perfect foods, it is possible to enjoy great eating, while keeping your cholesterol and weight under control without the pain of feeling deprived. Take it from us. We've done it, and you can, too.

Chapter 2

Breakfasts

An omelet is really scrambled eggs
enclosed in a coating of coagulated egg.
—Auguste Escoffier

Someone has probably told each of us that breakfast is the most important meal of the day, yet so many of us still neglect this lovely, healthy opening to the day. Certainly, the first excuse for treating this meal cursorily is lack of time, but our neglect of breakfast may also stem from boredom. These recipes make clear that just because the morning meal is part of your routine, it need not be routine.

The recipes are easy to make, and most take so little time to make that they can be incorporated into a busy weekday schedule. Many of the dishes will also serve as elegant centerpieces for a weekend family breakfast or a brunch for guests. The flavors and the combinations of ingredients are mouthwatering and will perk up many a bored palate.

These dishes have come a long way from the humble scrambled egg whites.

The Classic Egg White Omelet

Serves two

Egg whites lend themselves beautifully to the classic French-style folded omelet. Follow the simple steps below and you will be on your way to creating fine restaurant-quality omelets for you and yours.

A nine-inch nonstick skillet is the essential tool, and we find that using a silicone spatula works best. This version cooks slightly longer than the traditional French-style. We like our egg whites firm, not runny.

This recipe serves two people. Bear in mind that all fillings should be warm or at room temperature and fully cooked (with the exception of cheeses) before adding them.

INGREDIENTS:

> 6 egg whites
> salt and freshly ground pepper
> 1 teaspoon fresh chives or ¼ teaspoon dried
> ¼ cup sliced cooked mushrooms or shredded cheese or
> both (optional)

STEPS:

1. Whisk the egg whites with the salt and pepper in a small bowl until foamy.

2. Heat a nine-inch nonstick skillet over medium heat. Then spray the skillet with the cooking spray. Add the egg whites and let cook undisturbed for one minute. Using the spatula, lift the sides of the cooked egg white and allow the uncooked egg white to run underneath. Continue cooking until the top of the egg white is loosely set and sprinkle filling on top. With spatula, fold over half on top of itself. Cook one minute more. Slide onto a warmed platter and serve immediately.

The Perfect Poached White

Serves two

This is the method you will want to use for poached whites used in various recipes in this book (unless you own a special egg poacher pan) or to use on its own. Egg whites can be poached in advance and refrigerated for a day or so covered until ready to use. To reheat, just drop into simmering water for about thirty seconds.

INGREDIENTS:

4 egg whites, lightly beaten
1 teaspoon white vinegar

STEPS:

1. Into two cups of simmering water, add the white vinegar. Make a whirlpool in the water with a wooden spoon.

2. Drop two egg whites into the saucepan. Let set slightly and then drop in another two egg whites.

3. Poach four minutes until set. Remove with a slotted spoon and drain on kitchen towel or a paper towel. Serve immediately.

Cheesy Whites or Scrambled Whites

Serves two

Scrambled whites with tasty accoutrements are perhaps the simplest, most basic egg white dish of all. We eat them plain, but serving them with cheese alone, or cheese and herbs, turns ordinary comfort food into mouthwatering comfort food. Although ketchup is the traditional scrambled egg accompaniment, try using a flavored mustard or a spicy chutney instead.

INGREDIENTS:

> 8 egg whites, slightly beaten
> cooking spray
> ¼ cup low-fat cheese, shredded (optional)
> pinch dried oregano or herb of choice (optional)
> 1 tablespoon cream or low-fat cream for extra creaminess (optional)
> salt and pepper to taste

STEPS:

1. Heat a nine- to ten-inch nonstick skillet over medium-low heat. Spray the skillet with the cooking spray. Pour in the egg whites and let them set undisturbed for one minute. Stir slightly with a spatula, occasionally, for three minutes.

2. Add the cheese and herbs of your choice, stir, then season with salt and pepper to taste. Serve immediately.

   Here are some good mixers to add variety to your scrambled egg whites:

   • chopped tomatoes
   • sliced onion or scallions
   • shredded soy or veggie cheeses
   • capers, anchovies, pitted olives
   • leftover Brussels sprouts
   • diced chorizo, ham, or prosciutto

Smoked Salmon and Cream Cheese Scramble

Serves eight

You won't miss the bagel here—everything is included to satisfy your taste for a smoked salmon fix in this recipe. Make it in a large skillet and serve it right from there to the table. This is also a great centerpiece for a casual brunch.

INGREDIENTS:

> 24 egg whites, slightly beaten
>
> cooking spray
>
> salt and pepper to taste
>
> 6 ounces smoked salmon, cut into thin strips
>
> 4 ounces low-fat cream cheese
>
> 1 medium tomato, seeded and diced
>
> ½ small red onion, diced
>
> 2 tablespoons chopped fresh dill (for garnish)

STEPS:

1. Heat a large nonstick skillet over medium heat, spray with cooking spray. Add the egg whites and salt and pepper, stir lightly until they begin to set, about five to six minutes.

2. Add smoked salmon and spoon the cream cheese to sprinkle around the top. Sprinkle tomato and onion on top, cook another three to five minutes, then cover for two minutes more.

3. Uncover and garnish with the chopped dill and serve right from the skillet.

Matzo and Asparagus Omelet

Serves five to six

This dish can be served as part of a lunch or dinner. If you choose to make it without the vegetables, the dish is a traditional Jewish breakfast called matzo brie, and it's served with maple syrup. Experiment with other favorite fillings and combinations. The sky is your only limit.

INGREDIENTS:

> 1 teaspoon canola oil
>
> 1 medium onion, diced
>
> 2 cups asparagus, diced, about one medium-size bunch, blanched
>
> 3 sheets plain matzo, soaked in water to cover
>
> 16 egg whites
>
> salt and freshly ground black pepper

STEPS:

1. Heat the oil in a large nonstick skillet over medium heat. Add onion and sauté three to five minutes, stirring constantly. Add asparagus and sauté one minute more.

2. Squeeze excess water from matzo and add the matzo to skillet, stir to combine with the vegetables.

3. Stir egg whites until foamy in a separate bowl and add to the skillet.

4. Lift the edges of the cooked egg white with the spatula and allow uncooked white to flow to the bottom and sides of pan. Repeat this motion until all of the egg white is cooked, which will take about seven minutes.

5. Season with salt and pepper and slide onto a serving platter. Serve immediately.

Tortilla de Patata
or Spanish Potato Omelet

Serves six to eight

This is an egg-white version of the famous Spanish potato omelet that is served in tapas bars all over Spain. It's delicious hot or at room temperature, and makes a great hors d'oeuvre when cut into bite-size servings. This tortilla can also work as a terrific brunch dish or starter at a dinner party. A fino Spanish sherry complements it nicely.

INGREDIENTS:

> 16 egg whites
>
> 2 teaspoons salt
>
> ¼ teaspoon freshly ground black pepper
>
> 2 pounds Yukon gold potatoes
>
> 1 large Spanish onion
>
> 2 tablespoons olive oil
>
> 1 bunch watercress (for garnish), washed and trimmed

STEPS:

1. Beat egg whites until frothy in a large bowl, stir in salt and pepper. Set aside.

2. Wash and peel the potatoes and slice them on a mandoline or the slicing blade of a food processor into ¹/₈-inch slices. Set aside.

3. Slice onion into thin slices using the mandoline or a knife. Set aside.

4. Bring a large pot of salted water to a boil and place potatoes and onions in it. Cook for ten minutes and drain the potatoes and onions. Gently blot off excess water and reserve.

5. Add potato and onion mixture to egg mixture and stir to combine.

6. In a ten-inch skillet, heat the olive oil over medium heat, add egg and potato mixture in one layer in pan. Reduce heat and shake pan occasionally for eight to ten minutes, until the bottom is lightly browned and the top is just set.

7. Cover skillet with a plate and invert tortilla onto the plate. Slide the tortilla off the plate and back into the skillet and cook an additional ten minutes.

8. Transfer to a platter and either serve right away or let cool to room temperature. Slice into wedges and garnish platter with the watercress.

In Spain, a tortilla is an egg-based omelet, but in Central and South America, a tortilla is a corn- or flour-based flat pancake used to hold various fillings.

Cajun Dirty
White Frittata

Serves six

A frittata is actually an Italian-style omelet built with various, savory fillings. Our method of creating this dish starts on the stove top and finishes in a hot oven, but it doesn't take long to make. Frittatas can serve up to eight people easily and since they finish cooking in the oven, they make a very easy and practical choice for brunch or any party. A frittata may be served hot from the oven or at room temperature and will be tasty either way. This version brings one of our favorite Cajun dishes, dirty rice, together with egg whites to create a spectacular main course.

INGREDIENTS:

16 egg whites, slightly beaten

½ medium onion, diced

½ medium green pepper, diced

1 medium stalk celery, diced

1 teaspoon Cajun spice mixture (see below) or try a ready-mixed brand in the spice section of your supermarket

6 ounces Andouille sausage, diced

1 cup cooked white rice

⅓ bunch parsley, rinsed and stemmed (for garnish)

⅓ pound raw chicken livers (optional), roughly chopped

STEPS:

1. Heat oven to 350 degrees.

2. In a large nonstick ovenproof skillet, heat the olive oil. Add the onions, peppers, and celery and reduce heat to medium. Sauté five to seven minutes until the vegetables brown slightly, stirring occasionally. Add the Cajun spice mixture and stir to combine.

3. Add the andouille sausage (and chicken livers) and stir and sauté another five minutes, breaking up chicken livers into small pieces. Add cooked rice and stir to combine.

4. Add beaten egg whites. As the egg whites begin to cook, lift sides with the spatula, allowing the egg whites to set slightly for three minutes.

5. Remove from stove top and place in the oven (to ovenproof a rubber-handled skillet, mold two layers of aluminum foil around the handle for protection) for fifteen to eighteen minutes until firm and no liquid egg white remains.

6. Remove from the oven and invert onto a serving platter. Garnish with fresh parsley. Sprinkle one tablespoon or so of the Cajun spice mixture around the rim of the plate for garnish. Serve warm or at room temperature.

To make your own Cajun spice mixture, combine the following spices. This makes more than you need for this recipe so you can store the excess in a jar.

INGREDIENTS:

    2 teaspoons ground red pepper

    1 ½ teaspoons salt

    1 ½ teaspoons black pepper

    1 ¼ teaspoons sweet paprika

    1 teaspoon dry mustard powder

    1 teaspoon ground cumin

    1 teaspoon dried thyme

    1 teaspoon crushed oregano

Frittata Exotica

You can use the Cajun Dirty Rice recipe to build your own fritatta from your favorite ingredients, leftovers, or what you have on hand, such as meats, raw or cooked vegetables, or cheeses.

Baked Eggs with Prosciutto, Tomato, and Leeks

Serves eight

This dish is so simple to make and it can be prepared the night before. If you decide to wait and bake the dish in the morning, add the egg whites then, just before baking. It's a tasty and satisfying breakfast or luncheon meal for guests. Thinly sliced ham could be substituted for the prosciutto if you wish.

You may want to chop the tomatoes in the can by using kitchen shears and then drain them in a colander. This is a very quick and easy method.

INGREDIENTS:

2 28-ounce cans plum tomatoes, drained and chopped

2 tablespoons olive oil

1 teaspoon red wine vinegar

6 or 7 shakes of hot sauce (such as Tabasco)

¼ teaspoon celery seed

salt and freshly ground pepper

cooking spray

8 slices good-quality whole wheat bread

¼ pound proscuitto, sliced paper thin

14 egg whites

3 tablespoons heavy cream (optional)

3 tablespoons olive oil

2 medium leeks, trimmed, cleaned, and sliced into thin strips

STEPS:

1. Preheat oven to 375 degrees. In a medium-size bowl, combine the tomatoes, 2 tablespoons hot sauce olive oil, vinegar, celery seed, salt and pepper, and taste for seasoning.

2. Spray a nine- by thirteen-inch ovenproof baking dish with the cooking spray. Lay the bread slices in one layer to cover the bottom of the dish. Top with the prosciutto slices and then the tomato mixture. Make eight indentations with the

back of a large spoon in the tomato mixture and pour the egg whites over the top. Drizzle with the heavy cream if you are using it.

3. Cover with foil and bake thirty minutes or until the egg whites have set. Remove from the oven and set aside.

4. In a large skillet over medium heat, heat the 3 tablespoons olive oil and sauté the leeks eight to ten minutes, stirring constantly, until crispy brown. Drain on paper towels, sprinkle with some salt.

5. Garnish the dish with the crispy leeks and serve.

"Egg"plant Benedict

Serves three to six

When you or your family crave eggs Benedict, that culinary indulgence, try this delicious variation. It is very low in fat and just as satisfying, but with the added benefit of being easier to prepare. The egg white-only "hollandaise" provides the familiar tang and creaminess for this dish and it is versatile enough to be used in any recipe that calls for hollandaise sauce.

BENEDICT INGREDIENTS:

> cooking spray
>
> 1 large eggplant, sliced into 6 half-inch round slices
>
> 6 low-fat breakfast sausage patties (or vegetarian "sausage" patties)

MOCK HOLLANDAISE SAUCE:

> 1½ tablespoons cornstarch
>
> ½ teaspoon dry mustard
>
> ⅔ cup low-fat milk, or non-fat evaporated milk
>
> 2 egg whites
>
> 1 large lemon, juiced
>
> 4 tablespoons unsalted butter, melted (you may substitute a good
> canola butter/margarine)
>
> salt and pepper to taste
>
>
> 12 egg whites
>
> 2 tablespoons chopped fresh chives (for garnish)

STEPS:

1. Preheat the oven to 450 degrees and spray a baking tray with the cooking spray.

2. Place the eggplant slices in a colander, sprinkle liberally with salt, and allow to drain for twenty minutes. Wipe off the excess salt and moisture from each slice. Spread out the eggplant slices on the baking tray and spray liberally with the cooking spray. Place in oven eight to ten minutes until they start to brown. Turn

the slices over and spray again with the cooking spray. Bake another ten minutes. Remove and reserve, keeping them warm.

3. At the same time, place sausage patties on a baking tray and bake eight to ten minutes until browned. Remove from oven and keep warm.

4. To prepare hollandaise sauce: combine the cornstarch, dry mustard, milk, and egg whites in a small saucepan and cook over medium heat five to seven minutes, stirring constantly until thickened. Add lemon juice, butter, and salt and pepper and whisk to combine. Taste for seasoning and set aside. Keep warm until serving.

5. Poach the egg whites, using the method on page 26 or using an egg poacher. To use an egg poacher, boil water in the poacher, spray egg containers with cooking spray, add two egg whites per container, and cover and poach five to seven minutes until the whites are just set. Repeat with the remaining egg whites. Reserve.

6. To assemble the dish, place eggplant slices on a serving platter, top with sausage patties and poached egg whites, drizzle with several spoonfuls of the hollandaise sauce. Garnish with chopped chive and serve one to two eggplant Benedicts per guest.

Huevos Rancheros Blancos
or Mexican Ranch-Style Egg Whites

Serves six

This is a simple adaptation of a tried-and-true recipe. Trust us, you will not miss the yolk. We both love huevos rancheros and so had to adapt them to a pure egg-white scenario. We've modified this recipe so you can serve it to a crowd at a breakfast or lunch or even dinner. Serve this with lots of fresh hot flour or corn tortillas. The beans and ranchero salsa can be made the day ahead. The refried beans can be made using canned pinto beans; just remember to drain and rinse them before proceeding with the rest of the recipe.

> 16 egg whites
>
> 1 cup crumbled cotija (or ricotta salata) cheese

FOR THE REFRIED BEANS:

> 1 bag (16 ounces) dried pinto beans (or 2 15.5-ounce cans pinto beans, well rinsed and drained, liquid reserved)
>
> water to cover
>
> 1 whole medium onion, peeled
>
> 5 cloves garlic, peeled
>
> 2 tablespoons olive oil
>
> ½ medium onion, diced
>
> salt and pepper

STEPS:

1. Soak dried beans overnight in cold water to cover. Drain and place beans in a cooking pot with the whole onion and garlic and cover with fresh water. Cover and cook until the beans are soft; time will vary depending on the age of the bean, anywhere from one to two hours. Drain the beans and reserve the cooking liquid.

2. In a large nonstick skillet, heat the olive oil. Place the diced onion in the skillet and sauté until translucent, five to seven minutes, stirring occasionally. Add the drained, cooked beans or canned beans and sauté five minutes, stirring occasionally. Mash the beans-onion mixture with a potato masher or electric

wand blender, adding the bean liquid as necessary to create a soupy texture. Season with the salt and pepper to taste and set aside.

FOR THE SALSA:

cooking spray

2 garlic cloves, peeled

2 pounds fresh plum tomatoes, halved

5 fresh Serrano chilies, or dried chiles, reconstituted in water and drained

2 tablespoons chopped onion

2 tablespoons olive oil

salt

STEPS:

1. Heat the oven to 400 degrees. On a cookie sheet sprayed with cooking spray, place the garlic, tomatoes, and serrano chilies. Roast for fifteen to twenty minutes, turning them until they are blackened on all sides. Remove from the oven and let cool.

2. Wear rubber gloves and seed the chilies to reduce the amount of heat if you wish or place all the roasted ingredients in the bowl of a food processor or blender and process to combine.

3. In a large nonstick skillet, heat the olive oil over high heat and sauté the chopped onion about three minutes. Add the blended ingredients and cook over high heat until slightly reduced, about eight to ten minutes, stirring constantly. Season with salt to taste and set aside. Keep warm.

TO ASSEMBLE THE DISH:

1. Preheat oven to 350 degrees.

2. In a ten- by fifteen-inch casserole dish, spread the refried beans, covering the bottom. With the bottom of a soup ladle or large spoon, make eight indentations into the bean mixture.

3. Place two raw egg whites in each hole. Spread salsa over the whole dish and top with the cheese. Cover dish and bake for thirty-five to forty minutes, until the eggs are set and the beans are heated through. Serve with warmed corn or flour tortillas.

Smoked Turkey Hash
with Poached Whites

Serves four to six

This is an easy and great brunch dish because it can be made a day ahead. Any leftover cooked meat, such as corned beef, roast beef; or chicken; or fish, such as salmon, works in this dish, but we like smoked turkey the best because of its smoky saltiness.

INGREDIENTS:

2 teaspoons olive oil

1 medium yellow onion, diced

2 fresh carrots, peeled, and finely shredded

¼ head medium red cabbage, finely shredded

1 pound new potatoes, peeled, cooked, and diced

16 ounces smoked turkey, diced, about 3 cups

1 teaspoon caraway seeds

1 teaspoon balsamic vinegar

salt and freshly ground black pepper

12 egg whites

Mock hollandaise sauce (see recipe on page 36)

1 bunch watercress, washed and trimmed (for garnish)

STEPS:

1. In a large inch skillet over medium heat, add oil and onion and sauté (three to five minutes) until translucent, stirring occasionally. Add carrots and cabbage and sauté, stirring about two minutes. Add potatoes and turkey and sauté another two minutes, stirring. Add caraway seeds and vinegar and salt and pepper to taste and stir.

2. Press down on hash with the back of the spatula. Allow to cook undisturbed for ten minutes until brown. Flip over in sections with a spatula and allow to brown five to seven minutes more. Remove from heat and reserve warm.

3. Poach the egg whites, using the method described on page 26, or boil water in your egg poacher. Spray egg containers with cooking spray, add two egg whites per container, cover, and poach five to seven minutes until the whites are just set. Repeat with the remaining egg whites.

4. Place hash on serving platter or on individual plates, place egg whites on top, drizzle with the hollandaise sauce. Garnish with watercress and serve immediately.

Best-Ever Pancakes

Makes twelve pancakes

When we make these for our families, we always get a resounding "these pancakes are the best ever!" They cook up nice and fluffy and sometimes we add sliced bananas, blueberries, strawberries, sugared rhubarb, or thinly sliced apples. As you cook these pancakes, turn your oven on to 250 degrees. You can hold the platter of pancakes in the oven for about fifteen minutes or so at this temperature without drying them out.

INGREDIENTS:

> 1¼ cups whole wheat flour
> ¼ cup wheat germ
> 1 tablespoon brown sugar
> 3 teaspoons baking powder
> ½ teaspoon salt
> 2 egg whites, lightly beaten
> 1 cup low-fat milk
> 1 teaspoon vanilla extract
> 2 tablespoons canola oil
> 2 egg whites, whipped to stiff peaks
> cooking spray

STEPS:

1. In a large mixing bowl, sift the dry ingredients and stir to combine. In a small bowl, combine the liquid ingredients up to and including the canola oil. Stir the liquid into the dry ingredients to combine but do not overmix; batter will still be somewhat lumpy.

2. Using a spatula, fold the whipped egg whites into the batter a third at a time, taking care not to deflate the whites.

3. Spray the nonstick skillet or griddle with the cooking spray and heat over medium heat (a small drop of water should sizzle when dropped onto the skillet). Spoon a quarter cup batter for each pancake onto skillet or griddle. Cook over

medium heat for two to three minutes or until bubbles appear on the surface, flip and cook for another two to three minutes. Repeat with the remaining batter, spraying the skillet with the cooking spray as necessary.

During the spring Equinox, it is said that an egg will stand on its small end. Although some have reported success, it is not known whether such results were due to the Equinox or to that particular egg.

Cornmeal Waffles

Makes eight waffles

We like to make these delicious waffles all year round to remind us of summer when the corn is sweet and plentiful. To complement this dish, you might want to serve it with real maple syrup and a good breakfast sausage, such as a low-fat chicken or turkey sausage.

INGREDIENTS:

> 1 cup whole wheat flour
>
> 1 cup finely ground yellow or white cornmeal
>
> 2 teaspoons baking powder
>
> ½ teaspoon baking soda
>
> 3 tablespoons brown sugar
>
> ½ teaspoon salt
>
> 3 tablespoons canola oil
>
> 2 cups buttermilk
>
> 4 egg whites
>
> 1 cup corn kernels (fresh when available, or reconstituted, dried, or thawed frozen)

STEPS:

1. Heat a waffle iron until a drop of water sizzles on its surface.

2. In a large bowl, combine the flour, cornmeal, baking powder, baking soda, brown sugar, and salt, and whisk.

3. Combine the oil, buttermilk, and egg whites in a small bowl and whisk.

4. Add the liquid ingredients to the dry ingredients, stir in the corn kernels, and stir to combine.

5. Spray the waffle iron with the cooking spray and pour half a cup of batter into the center of the waffle iron, close the lid, and wait for the steaming to stop. Remove the waffle and serve immediately. If you can't serve immediately, keep each waffle warm on a heatproof platter in the oven heated to 250 degrees. Repeat with the remaining batter, spraying the waffle iron as necessary with the cooking spray.

Fluffy Banana Waffles
with Coconut Syrup

Makes eight waffles

Whipped egg whites make these banana waffles so fluffy and light. This version is filled with fresh banana slices and shredded coconut, crispy on the outside and served with a warm creamy coconut syrup. Unsweetened flaked coconut can be found in the frozen food section of the supermarket.

INGREDIENTS:

> 6 egg whites
> pinch of salt
> ¼ teaspoon cream of tartar
> 1 cup unbleached flour
> 1 cup whole wheat flour
> ¼ cup unsweetened flaked coconut
> 1 teaspoon baking soda
> pinch of salt
> 2 teaspoons baking powder
> 4 tablespoons canola oil
> 2 cups buttermilk
> 1 13.5-ounce can sweetened coconut milk
> cooking spray
> 2 whole medium ripe bananas, sliced on the diagonal about
>   half an inch thick

STEPS:

1. Heat the waffle iron, until a drop of water sizzles on its surface.

2. Beat the egg whites with the salt and cream of tartar in a medium bowl until stiff.

3. Combine the flours, coconut, baking soda, baking powder, and salt in a large bowl. Stir with a whisk to combine.

4. Combine the oil and buttermilk in a small bowl and stir. Add the liquid ingredients

to the dry and stir. Fold in the stiffly beaten egg whites until just combined.

5. Pour the coconut milk into a small saucepan and heat over medium heat, stirring occasionally for five minutes. Reduce heat and keep warm.

6. Spray the waffle iron with the cooking spray. Pour half a cup batter into center of iron, allow to spread a bit, and add four slices of banana. Close lid and wait for the steaming to stop. Open the iron and remove the waffle. Serve immediately. Repeat with remaining batter, spraying the iron surface with cooking spray as necessary. To keep the waffles warm, place them on an ovenproof platter in an oven heated to 250 degrees.

Flavored French Toast

Serves six to eight

Flavored French toast will provide an almost unlimited variety to your breakfast menu without unnecessary fuss. You can use the following extracts found in the spice section of your local supermarket. Mix and match them to find your favorite flavor combination. These toasts are made with no added fat. They're especially healthful when served with low-fat yogurt and sliced fresh fruit or a quick fruit compote (see recipe below).

INGREDIENTS:

> 10 egg whites
> 1 teaspoon pure vanilla extract (or your choice of extract)
> 1 teaspoon orange extract (optional)
> ¼ cup plus 2 tablespoons non-fat milk or non-fat evaporated
>   skimmed milk
> pinch of salt
> 8 slices good quality sandwich bread or baguette
> cooking spray

STEPS:

1. Combine egg whites, extracts, milk, and salt in a medium-sized bowl and whisk to mix. Add a slice of bread and soak briefly, turning over once and squeezing out excess.

2. Heat a ten-inch nonstick skillet over medium heat and coat with cooking spray.

3. Add as many slices of bread as will comfortably fit in the skillet or on the stovetop griddle, but do not crowd the pan. Cook three to five minutes and turn the slices and cook another three minutes more. Remove from skillet and reserve warm. You can keep them warm on an ovenproof platter in an oven set to 250 degrees.

FRUIT COMPOTE:
Makes 1¼ cups

14 pitted prunes, apricots, or dried figs

2 tablespoons sliced almonds

1 teaspoon cinnamon

1 cup prune juice or water

1 vanilla bean (or 1 teaspoon pure vanilla extract)

2 tablespoons brown sugar (optional)

STEPS:

1. Combine ingredients in a medium saucepan over medium heat, add additional water to cover fruit, and simmer for ten to twelve minutes until slightly thickened and the liquid has reduced.

2. Remove vanilla bean and reserve for another use.

3. Keep compote warm.

Keep the French Toast, Lose the Fat

Use a George Foreman grill to make a tasty, healthy, and simple version of traditional French toast with no added fat. Just place the flavored egg white–soaked bread in a heated grill, close lid, and let cook for three to four minutes.

Chapter 3

Tasty Shakes for Breakfast or Any Time of the Day

Probably one of the most private things in the world is an egg until it is broken.
—M.F.K. Fisher

Make these tasty egg white–based shakes at home. There is no need to frequent those pricey health food juice bars when, with just a couple of fresh ingredients and a blender, food processor, or cocktail shaker, you can create delicious drinks at home. Use these recipes as springboards to invent your own "signature" shake. They will satisfy you until your next meal.

Cold Cappuccino Shake

Makes one serving

This makes a great summertime drink. It can work well with breakfast or lunch or all on its own. Make sure to use a pasteurized egg-white product (such as All Whites) in this recipe as the whites will not be cooked.

INGREDIENTS:

> 4 ounces egg whites, such as All Whites
>
> ¼ teaspoon instant espresso (decaf or regular) granules
>
> 2 tablespoons non-fat dried milk powder
>
> ¼ teaspoon cinnamon
>
> 2 ice cubes
>
> 2 tablespoons cold water

STEP:

Combine all ingredients in the blender and blend well.

Cowboy Coffee

The cowboys out west on the range used to throw some crushed egg shells into the pot with a few handfuls of coffee and water, boil up the mixture, strain out the shells, and drink it. They were employing a crude method of clarifying a cloudy or bitter liquid with egg shells and the bits of protein that were clinging to them. This is similar to the method used today to clarify beef and chicken stocks (see recipe for Chicken Consommé on page 68)

Eggs on the Go Breakfast Shake

Makes one generous serving.

Don't have time to cook your egg-white omelet this morning? Try this nutritionally packed shake. It's got it all: calcium, vitamin C, protein, and great taste. You won't even miss the coffee or bagel. Make sure to use a pasteurized egg-white product.

INGREDIENTS:

> 2 ounces egg whites, such as All Whites
> 3 large strawberries, washed and hulled
> 1 cup orange juice
> 1½ tablespoons non-fat powdered milk
> 2 ice cubes

Put all the ingredients in the blender and blend well.

Avocado Carrot Shake

Makes one generous serving

This veggie shake is so rich and creamy, it will make you feel like you've had a real treat, as well as a healthy one. Florida avocados, the bright green ones, are the best ones to use here as they contain more water in their flesh and make for a juicier drink.

INGREDIENTS:

> 2 ounces egg whites, such as All Whites
> ½ very ripe medium avocado, peeled and seeded
> ¼ cup fresh squeezed carrot juice (or apple juice)
> 2 ice cubes

Combine all ingredients in the blender and blend well.

Fruit Yogurt Shake

Makes enough for one generous serving

Our kids enjoy these as much as we do. They are packed with vitamins and protein for an excellent quickie lunch, after-school snack, or on-the-go breakfast for anyone. For a variation, use berries, peaches, kiwi, or any other of your favorite fresh or frozen fruits.

INGREDIENTS:

1 banana

4 ounces egg whites, such as All Whites

¼ cup plain non-fat yogurt

2 tablespoons honey

1 ice cube

STEP:

Place all ingredients in a blender and blend well.

Chapter 4

Muffins, Quickbreads, and Side Dishes

Nothing like the little courses to make a tasty morsel.

—Anonymous

These are the stand-by recipes in any kitchen, the ones that you can serve at almost any meal and any time in between, as well. We've used egg whites to lighten and enhance the flavors of some of your favorites and created some brand-new dishes. The muffins and breads freeze well.

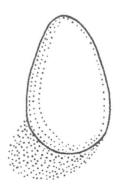

Pumpkin Ginger Muffins

Makes a dozen muffins

These delicious and moist muffins are great any time of the day. They're not too sweet, are packed with pumpkin and candied ginger, and can still satisfy a late-day craving.

INGREDIENTS:

cooking spray

1¼ cups whole wheat flour

1 cup rolled oats

1 tablespoon baking powder

½ teaspoon salt

½ teaspoon ground cinnamon

1½ teaspoons pumpkin pie spice

3 tablespoons crystallized ginger, minced finely

¼ cup brown sugar

3 egg whites

1 cup canned unsweetened pumpkin purée

½ cup evaporated skimmed milk

½ cup apple juice or prune juice

2 tablespoons canola oil

STEPS:

1. Preheat the oven to 375 degrees.

2. Prepare the twelve-muffin tin by placing paper cupcake liners in place and spraying lightly with the cooking spray.

3. Sift the dry ingredients in a large mixing bowl and stir with a whisk to combine. In a small mixing bowl, combine the liquid ingredients and stir. Add the liquid mixture to the dry mixture, stirring with a wooden spoon just to combine.

4. Spoon batter into the prepared muffin tin and bake twenty to twenty-five minutes, until a toothpick inserted into the center of a muffin comes out clean. Remove from oven and let cool ten minutes. Remove muffins from tin and let cool on a rack.

Strawberry Muffins

Makes a dozen muffins

These muffins with their lovely pink color help make any breakfast table more beautiful. Be sure to have plenty on hand because their appeal will have folks asking for more. Peaches and nectarines are delicious substitutions for the strawberries.

INGREDIENTS:

cooking spray

1¼ cups whole wheat flour

¼ cup wheat germ

2½ teaspoons baking powder

1 teaspoon ground cinnamon

¼ cup brown sugar

¼ teaspoon salt

²/₃ cup non-fat vanilla yogurt (one 6-ounce container)

2 tablespoons oil

½ cup evaporated skimmed milk

2 egg whites

1½ cups strawberries, washed and chopped fine (fresh or frozen)

2 tablespoons brown sugar

½ teaspoon cinnamon

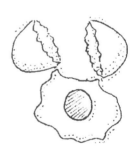

STEPS:

1. Preheat the oven to 375 degrees.

2. Prepare the twelve-muffin tin by placing paper cupcake liners in place and spraying with a light coating of cooking spray.

3. Place the dry ingredients in a large mixing bowl and stir with a whisk to combine. Combine the yogurt, oil, milk, and egg whites in a small mixing bowl and stir with a whisk to combine. Add the liquid ingredients to the dry, stirring just to combine.

4. In another small mixing bowl, combine the strawberries with the brown sugar and cinnamon and mix to combine.

5. Spoon the batter into the muffin tins halfway, top each with two to three teaspoons of the strawberry mixture and bake for twenty-five minutes until a tester inserted into the center of a muffin comes out clean. Remove from oven and let cool ten minutes. Remove muffins from tin and let cool on a rack.

That Darn Tarnish

The sulfur in egg whites will definitely tarnish your silverware. We like to use disposable tarnish-cleaning cloths on our tarnished utensils.

Banana Almond Muffins

Makes a dozen muffins

These make a great mid-morning or late-afternoon snack. If you bake up a batch, they make a nice accompaniment to a school lunch or a tasty and healthy coffee-break treat at the office. Try spraying the measuring cup with cooking spray before measuring out the honey to prevent it from sticking.

INGREDIENTS:

cooking spray
1¾ cups whole wheat flour
1 cup rolled oats
¼ cup brown sugar
1 tablespoon baking powder
¾ cup sliced almonds
1 teaspoon cinnamon
½ teaspoon salt
3 bananas, mashed
4 egg whites, lightly beaten
1 cup plain low-fat yogurt
3 tablespoons oil
¼ cup honey

STEPS:

1. Preheat the oven to 375 degrees.

2. Prepare a twelve-muffin tin by placing paper cupcake liners in place and spraying them lightly with cooking spray.

3. Place the dry ingredients in a large mixing bowl and stir with a whisk to combine. Combine the bananas, egg whites, yogurt, oil, and honey in a smaller mixing bowl and stir with a whisk. Pour the liquid ingredients into the dry and stir to combine.

4. Spoon into the prepared muffin tin. Bake eighteen to twenty minutes or until a tester inserted into the center of a muffin comes out clean. Remove from the oven and let cool ten minutes. Remove muffins from tin and let cool on a rack.

Zucchini Corn Bread

Serves nine

Two favorite summer flavors are combined in this recipe to produce a light moist corn bread which can be enjoyed any time of the day. This healthier version of traditional corn bread is great as a breakfast bread, but is also a wonderful accompaniment served with the Black and White Chili on page 110 or the Texas-Style Meatloaf on page 126.

INGREDIENTS:

> cooking spray
> 1 cup finely ground yellow or white cornmeal
> 1 cup oat flour
> ⅓ cup brown sugar
> 2½ teaspoons baking powder
> ½ teaspoon salt
> ½ cup rolled oats
> 1 cup grated, unpeeled raw zucchini
> 1 cup buttermilk
> 5 tablespoons melted butter or margarine, cooled
> 4 egg whites

STEPS:

1. Preheat oven to 400 degrees. Spray a nine-inch square baking pan with the cooking spray.

2. Place the cornmeal, oat flour, brown sugar, baking powder, and salt into a medium bowl and stir with a whisk to combine. Add the rolled oats and zucchini and stir. In a small bowl, combine the buttermilk, butter, and egg whites; whisk to combine.

3. Add the liquid ingredients to the dry and stir to combine. Pour into the prepared pan and bake for twenty-five minutes or until lightly browned and a tester inserted in the middle of the bread comes out clean.

Spoonbread

Serves six

For breakfast served alone, or as a luncheon meal when served with a salad, or a quick and easy side dish at dinner, you can't beat the versatility of spoonbread. This is similar to a soufflé in texture and will rise elegantly and fall just as quickly, so serve it immediately.

INGREDIENTS:

> cooking spray
> 1½ cups boiling water
> 1 cup finely ground yellow or white cornmeal
> 1 tablespoon butter
> 3 egg whites, unbeaten
> 1 cup buttermilk
> 1 teaspoon salt
> 1 teaspoon sugar
> 1 teaspoon baking powder
> ¼ teaspoon baking soda
> 3 egg whites, whipped to soft peaks

STEPS:

1. Preheat the oven to 375 degrees. Spray a two-quart baking dish with the cooking spray.

2. In a medium saucepan over medium heat, bring the water to a boil and stir in the cornmeal with a whisk. Add the butter, unbeaten egg whites, buttermilk, salt, sugar, baking powder, and baking soda and stir thirty seconds. Remove from heat and transfer mixture to a large mixing bowl. Fold in the whipped egg whites one-third at a time, being careful not to deflate them.

3. Transfer the mixture to the prepared baking dish and bake for forty-five to fifty minutes, until puffed and golden. Remove from the oven and serve immediately.

Butternut Squash Soufflé

Makes four servings

Soufflés seem scary to make, but once you try, you'll find they really aren't difficult at all. The whipped egg whites work their magic right before your eyes. You don't even need a soufflé dish; any fairly shallow ovenproof dish will do the trick. Just follow the simple rules here and you'll be on your way to incorporating soufflés into your everyday meals.

It is a fallacy that loud voices in the kitchen will make your soufflé fall. The most important thing is that it must go from oven to table in minutes so everyone can ooh and ahh about the triumph of that highfalutin soufflé. By the way, it tastes just as delicious after it falls a bit, but is not quite as pretty to serve. Trust us, many a soufflé has fallen over the years, but none has gone uneaten.

INGREDIENTS:

> 2 tablespoons plus 1 teaspoon unsalted butter
> 2 tablespoons flour
> ½ cup non-fat milk, room temperature
> ¼ teaspoon salt
> freshly ground black pepper
> 1 shallot, finely minced
> pinch of salt
> 1 cup butternut squash purée (from a 12-ounce package frozen
>   squash, drained)
> ¼ teaspoon nutmeg
> 2 teaspoons finely minced fresh sage leaves
> 4 egg whites
> ¼ teaspoon cream of tartar
> pinch of salt

STEPS:

1. Preheat the oven to 400 degrees.

2. Prepare a one-quart ovenproof dish by buttering the inside and coating it with

one tablespoon breadcrumbs or grated Parmesan cheese. Refrigerate it until ready to fill it.

3. Melt two tablespoons butter in skillet over medium heat. When the butter is foamy, stir in flour, keep stirring, one minute or a little more, then whisk in the milk. Cook, stirring constantly, over low heat until the sauce becomes thickened. Season to taste with salt and pepper and set aside.

4. In a small skillet, sauté the shallot in one teaspoon butter and a pinch of salt until just translucent, about one to two minutes and set aside.

5. Place the butternut squash purée in a large bowl. Add the butter-flour mixture, the shallots, nutmeg, sage, and salt and pepper. Taste and adjust seasoning.

6. In a clean mixing bowl, beat the egg whites with the cream of tartar and salt until stiff peaks form.

7. Add one-third of the beaten egg whites to the squash mixture and stir to combine. Fold in half the remaining egg whites until combined and then fold in the other half, taking care not to deflate the whites.

8. Pour into the prepared pan and bake immediately for twenty-five to thirty minutes.

Rules for Making your Soufflé

1. Properly prepare your pan by buttering it and patting the sides with breadcrumbs—the egg whites need something "to climb."

2. Beat your egg whites thoroughly until very stiff.

3. Season your base and taste it before you add the beaten egg whites.

4. The proper way to fold in the egg whites is to lighten the base first by adding one-third of the beaten egg whites and mixing it thoroughly. Then fold in the rest of the whites one half at a time by using a spatula and holding it vertically, using a downward stroke and turning the bowl a half turn as you bring up the spatula.

5. Bake it in a hot oven. It is done when it has risen two to three inches above the level at which it went into the oven.

6. Rush it—and your guests—to the table when it has risen high and mighty.

Sunchoke and Potato Pancakes

Makes eight to ten pancakes

Sunchokes, also called Jerusalem artichokes, are available in the produce section of the market and resemble ginger root in appearance. The tuber of the sunflower plant, they taste like a cross between a potato, jicama, and an artichoke. We came up with the idea of a virtuous, no-oil potato-sunchoke pancake and it is delicious. Serve them with a non-fat sour cream and some mango chutney.

INGREDIENTS:

> 12 ounces peeled red-skinned potatoes, grated, about 1½ cups, well packed
> 12 ounces peeled sunchokes, grated, about 1½ cups, well packed
> ½ small onion, grated
> 3 egg whites
> 1 teaspoon salt
> ¼ teaspoon freshly ground pepper
> cooking spray

STEPS:

1. Combine potatoes, sunchokes, and onions and place into a kitchen towel and wring out tightly to get rid of excess moisture. If you are going to hold these for a time before cooking, you will need to soak them in water as they discolor in minutes when exposed to air. Then you will need to wring out the excess moisture again.

2. In a large mixing bowl, add the onions and potato mixture, egg whites, salt and freshly ground black pepper, and mix to combine.

3. In a large size nonstick skillet over high heat, spray with cooking spray. Add a quarter-cup of potato-sunchoke mixture into the skillet, pressing down with a spatula. You can make four at a time in a large skillet.

4. Cook five minutes over high heat, until browned. Turn the pancakes over and cover the skillet for three minutes. Remove the cover and cook for an additional three minutes. Transfer them to a heated serving platter and reserve.

5. Spray the skillet with the cooking spray and repeat with remaining mixture.

As a variation, try substituting the sunchokes with the following:

- sweet potatoes
- parsnips
- carrots
- jicama

Zucchini Pancakes

Makes six pancakes

These pancakes couldn't be simpler to make as a breakfast treat or light lunch. As a side dish for dinner, these make a great low-carb alternative to potato pancakes. You may want to experiment and add some grated onion and/or Parmesan cheese to the recipe for variation.

INGREDIENTS:

> 1½ cups grated, unpeeled fresh zucchini
> 1 tablespoon cornstarch
> 4 egg whites
> 2 teaspoons salt
> ¼ teaspoon pepper
> cooking spray

STEPS:

1. In a medium mixing bowl, combine the zucchini, cornstarch, egg whites, and salt and freshly ground black pepper.

2. Spray a large nonstick skillet with cooking spray and heat over medium heat. Spoon a quarter-cup zucchini mixture into skillet for each pancake. You can make four at a time in a large skillet. Cook four minutes; turn over and cook another three to four minutes until lightly browned.

3. Remove from skillet and serve immediately. Repeat with remaining batter.

Chapter 5
Soups

*A hen is only an egg's way of
making another egg.*
—Samuel Butler

We've put together a group of versatile recipes
for soups, salads, and sandwiches that offer you
a lot of easy ways to pair soups and sandwiches, and soups
and salads, for varied and original luncheons or entrées.

Egg whites work well in soups. After all, egg drop soup
is an international favorite, and it doesn't take much effort
to create some delicious variations. The soups we've created
can work as light entrées with a crusty bread, a cheese board,
and one of the salads, or they may be served as a first course
at a more elaborate meal.

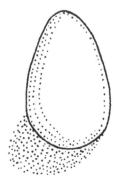

Chicken Consommé

Serves six to eight

The egg whites used in this recipe are not eaten but perform a rather interesting task when combined with common homemade chicken stock, clarifying it into a beautiful, golden, crystal-clear soup. This is a fun cooking project to do with your kids and fellow cooking buffs. They will be fascinated with the result.

INGREDIENTS:

> 8 cups homemade chicken stock (see page 69)
>
> 8 egg whites and their shells
>
> 2 carrots, sliced into paper-thin slices
>
> 2 stalks celery, sliced into paper-thin slices
>
> 1 scallion, sliced into paper thin slices

STEPS:

1. Pour the chicken stock into a large saucepan.

2. Beat the egg whites lightly and add them with their crushed shells to the saucepan. Over low heat, stir the mixture to circulate the egg whites into the stock. Bring the stock to a simmer and let simmer for five to ten minutes.

3. Remove from the heat and let mixture stand for fifteen minutes while the whites and shells rise to the top of the pan, forming a raft-like structure.

4. Line a colander with dampened cheesecloth. Pour the stock through and let drip slowly, undisturbed, until only the egg-white raft remains. Discard the egg whites and shells.

5. Pour the clear stock back into a clean saucepan and add the vegetables. Bring the mixture to a simmer and let vegetables cook five to eight minutes until barely tender. Taste for seasoning and add salt and pepper if needed. Ladle into shallow bowls and serve.

Basic Chicken Stock

Makes about three quarts

INGREDIENTS:

    5 pounds chicken wings

    6 quarts cold water

    1 small bunch fresh parsley

    2 whole bay leaves

    2 ribs celery, halved

    2 carrots, peeled and roughly chopped

    2 onions, peeled and quartered

    1 whole head garlic, unpeeled

STEPS:

1. Rinse the chicken parts to remove any blood. Place them in the bottom of a heavy-duty, large (ten-quart) stockpot. Cover with six quarts cold water.

2. Place stockpot on the stove over high heat. Bring to a boil, reduce heat, and simmer for five to ten minutes, skimming the thick foam that rises to the top with a slotted spoon and discard. Never stir the stock.

3. Make a bouquet garni by tying the parsley and bay leaves inside the celery stalks. Add all the vegetables to the pot and let the stock simmer undisturbed and uncovered for three to four hours. The stock will reduce by about one half.

4. Remove from the heat and strain through a layer of dampened cheesecloth set in a colander. Refrigerate until the fat congeals and skim off the fat that rises to the top. The stock can be frozen in small amounts at this point or held in the refrigerator for two days. The stock freezes beautifully. You can freeze it in batches in small containers to use in soups and sauces.

Winemakers use egg shells and bits of egg white to clarify their product during the winemaking process.

Beef Consommé

Serves six to eight

This recipe for a delicious and healthful soup is a good one to have in your cooking repertoire. The homemade beef stock needed for this recipe will perfume your kitchen when you are making it and our butcher always shares his extra bones with us, an added bonus.

INGREDIENTS:

> 8 cups homemade beef stock (see page 71)
> 8 egg whites and their shells
> 2 carrots, sliced into paper-thin slices
> 2 stalks, celery sliced into paper-thin slices
> 1 scallion, sliced into paper-thin slices

STEPS:

1. Pour the beef stock into a large saucepan. Beat the egg whites lightly and add them with their crushed shells to the saucepan. Over low heat, stir the mixture to circulate the egg whites into the stock. Bring the stock to a simmer and let simmer five to ten minutes. Remove from the heat and let mixture stand for fifteen minutes while the whites and shells rise to the top of the pan, forming a raft-like structure.

2. Line a colander with dampened cheesecloth. Pour the stock through and let it drip slowly, undisturbed until only the egg-white raft remains. Discard the egg whites and shells.

3. Pour the clear stock back into a clean saucepan and add the vegetables. Bring the mixture to a simmer and let vegetables cook five to eight minutes until barely tender. Taste for seasoning and add salt and pepper if needed.

4. Ladle into shallow bowls and serve.

Homemade Beef Stock

Makes three quarts
INGREDIENTS:

> 7 pounds beef (soup) bones
> 2 carrots, peeled and halved
> 2 medium onions, peeled and halved, studded with five whole cloves
> ½ head unpeeled garlic
> 2 celery stalks
> 2 leeks, washed and trimmed
> bouquet garni (half a bunch parsley, cleaned, 2 bay leaves, and
>   1 bunch thyme)
> 2 teaspoons salt
> 2 tablespoons Gravy Master (optional)

STEPS:

1. Heat oven to 450 degrees and roast the bones in a large roasting pan, turning every ten minutes. After twenty minutes, add the vegetables, except the bouquet garni, and cook an additional forty minutes. Do not let the vegetables burn. Remove from the oven.

2. Put the browned ingredients in the stockpot.

3. Deglaze the roasting pan on top of the stove by placing the roasting pan on top of one or two burners, with about one cup of water and pour this over the bones.

4. Pour this into a stockpot, add the bouquet garni and salt, cover with water, and bring to a boil. Skim off scum. Continue simmering four to six hours, adding more water to maintain the water level.

5. Strain the stock into another large bowl and cool immediately in the refrigerator. Skim off the fat and taste for seasonings. If the flavor is not robust enough, put back onto the stove and reduce to concentrate its strength. Add the Gravy Master now, if you have chosen to use it. Like the chicken stock, this stock freezes beautifully.

Egg White Drop Soup

Serves six

This is our version of egg drop soup with egg whites and a few twists. It can be made with white fish fillets, such as flounder or snapper, in place of the ground pork, or you can use ground turkey or beef. Try your favorite combination of ingredients to make it your own. It is simple and hearty and a weeknight favorite with our families. This is so much better when made with homemade chicken stock, but canned stock can be used. You might have to adjust the soy sauce so it's not too salty. We recommend using fresh egg whites in this soup as their gelatinous quality really adds richness to this soup. Omit the cilantro if you are not a fan, and use parsley instead.

INGREDIENTS:

> 6 cups chicken stock
>
> 3 slices of ginger, half an inch thick
>
> 1 tablespoon Schezuan peppercorns (optional)
>
> ¾ pound ground pork
>
> 1 cup peas
>
> ¼ pound chopped shrimp
>
> 3 tablespoons soy sauce
>
> 3 tablespoons minced scallions
>
> 2 tablespoons cornstarch
>
> 4 egg whites, beaten
>
> 1 cup chopped cilantro (or parsley) as a condiment
>
> chili oil (optional) as a condiment

STEPS:

1. Put all but a quarter cup of the stock in a large saucepan. Tie the ginger and peppercorns in a small piece of cheesecloth and add to the stock in the pan, along with the ground pork.

2. Bring to a boil, reduce heat, and simmer ten minutes. Skim any foam that might rise to the top.

3. Add peas, shrimp, soy sauce and scallions. Simmer five minutes. Remove cheesecloth pouch and discard.

4. In a small bowl, mix a quarter cup of stock with the cornstarch.

5. Drizzle egg whites slowly into the simmering soup in the saucepan, stirring constantly. Stir in cornstarch mixture. When mixture thickens, taste soup for seasoning. Add more soy sauce if necessary.

6. Serve with plenty of chopped cilantro and chili oil.

Thousand-Year-Old Eggs

These Chinese eggs are not really a thousand years old, but they are at least several years old. They are exempt from inspection and grading and are quite remarkably edible. The taste ranges from salty to wine-like to a citrus flavor.

Tomato Egg White Drop Soup

Serves six to eight

We tried this soup at an Asian restaurant and liked it so much that we experimented and adjusted the ingredients over and over until we were satisfied with our own version. We think you'll love the result. Using fresh egg whites out of the shell provides the best result but you can use your favorite egg-white product. This soup can have quite a bite to it. If you're not a fan of spicy food, adjust the quantity of hot peppers or eliminate them altogether.

INGREDIENTS:

> 1 onion, chopped
> ½ fennel bulb, diced
> 1 28-ounce can whole plum tomatoes, drained
> 4 cups chicken stock (homemade or canned)
> 1 teaspoon fennel seeds
> 1 or 2 (to taste) fresh or dried hot peppers, seeded and minced
> ½ lemon, juiced
> ¼ cup Pernod (or other anise-flavored liquor)
> salt and pepper to taste
> 6 egg whites, slightly beaten

STEPS:

1. Heat enough oil in a large stockpot over medium heat to sauté the onion and fennel five to seven minutes until they begin to turn translucent.

2. Add the plum tomatoes and stir, breaking them up with a wooden spoon slightly, then add the chicken stock, fennel seed, and hot peppers. Cook over medium-low heat for thirty minutes.

3. Add lemon juice, Pernod, and salt and pepper and taste to correct seasonings.

4. Slowly pour in the egg whites and allow them to set for thirty seconds. Stir, breaking them up slightly, and cook another two minutes. Serve immediately.

Swiss Chard
and Egg White Soup

Serves six

Egg white noodles and fresh Swiss chard are the stars of this hearty soup. A vegetable stock or chicken stock could be substituted for the homemade beef broth, or you could use canned broth.

INGREDIENTS:

- 4 egg whites
- 5 teaspoons freshly grated Parmesan cheese
- ¼ teaspoon kosher salt
- pinch freshly ground black pepper
- 1 tablespoon all-purpose flour
- 6 cups homemade beef stock (see page 71)
- 1 pound Swiss chard, stemmed and sliced very thinly across

STEPS:

1. In a small bowl, mix together the egg whites, Parmesan cheese, salt, pepper, and flour.

2. In a medium saucepan, bring the stock to a boil. Place a colander over the saucepan and pour the egg mixture into it, letting it fall through the holes into the simmering broth. Stir the soup a bit and add the Swiss chard, stirring once or twice. Cook two to three minutes. Taste for seasoning and adjust if necessary. Serve immediately.

Joyce's Escarole and Egg White Soup

Serves six

This recipe came to us through our good friend, Joyce Engelson, a legendary book editor, author, and a great cook. Joyce insists that the tartness of the lemon makes salt unnecessary and we agree.

INGREDIENTS:

2 shallots, minced

1 medium head escarole, washed and chopped

3 tablespoons olive oil

3½ cups chicken stock homemade (see page 69)

1 raw boneless chicken breast, diced

1 lemon, juiced

5 tablespoons Parmesan cheese

7 egg whites, beaten slightly

STEPS:

1. Place the olive oil and shallots in a large saucepan over medium heat and sauté them three minutes until translucent. Add the chopped escarole and sauté for three to four minutes.

2. Add half a cup of the chicken stock and the diced chicken. Cover the saucepan, reduce the heat to low, and simmer for fifteen minutes. Add the remaining stock and simmer for ten minutes. Remove from the heat.

3. Whisk together the lemon juice and the cheese in a small bowl. Add to the saucepan and stir. Add the egg whites slowly and let them set for thirty seconds. Stir once or twice and serve immediately.

Duck eggs are oilier and richer in flavor than chicken eggs. When duck eggs are boiled, the yolk turns a red-orange while the white turns a bluish color.

Greek Egg Lemon Soup

Serves six to eight

This is the Greek version of chicken soup called *avgolemono*—a rich chicken stock thickened and flavored with egg whites, lemon, and orzo. Making this soup work requires a method called tempering. You ladle out a small amount of the hot liquid into the eggs—being careful not to scramble or cook them—thus raising the temperature of the liquid gradually. Then you add this mixture back into the hot stock.

Egg Beaters brand of egg white lends an extra richness to this soup.

INGREDIENTS:

> 6 cups chicken stock (preferably homemade; see page 69)
> ¼ cup uncooked orzo
> 1 cup liquid Egg Beaters
> ¼ cup plus 2 tablespoons lemon juice
> salt and freshly ground black pepper to taste

STEPS:

1. Bring the chicken stock to a boil in a medium saucepan over medium heat. Add the orzo and cook five to seven minutes until tender. Reduce heat and let soup simmer.

2. In a small bowl, combine the egg whites (Egg Beaters) and lemon juice. Ladle out half a cup of hot chicken stock into the egg mixture and whisk to combine. Pour this mixture back into the saucepan and stir three to five minutes until soup thickens; do not allow soup to boil. Season to taste with salt and pepper and serve hot.

Chapter 6
Salads

Egg salad is one of summer's greatest gifts.
—Anonymous

As a dish, salads provide a versatility few other dishes can. Basically, any ingredients can work in a salad, as long as you pair the right ones together. The easy, light flavor of egg whites make them a perfect host in a salad built with more piquant ingredients.

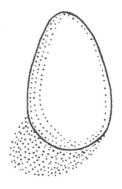

The Egg White Caesar Salad

Serves four to six

The traditional way to make the classic Caesar salad is to use a large wooden salad bowl. You begin by rubbing a whole garlic clove on the inside of the bowl, in preparation for mixing the salad tableside. Most of us have seen this dish prepared with much flair in various restaurants, and it looks more daunting than it really is as a dish—so don't be intimidated, and try this when you have the time. Egg Beaters brand of egg whites lend a creaminess to the Caesar dressing. Use top-quality ingredients and Caesar (and your assembled guests) will hail you.

INGREDIENTS:

  1 tablespoon minced garlic

  ½ teaspoon anchovy paste

  1 teaspoon Dijon mustard

  4 ounces egg-white product (such as Egg Beaters or any other
  pasteurized egg-white product)

  2 tablespoons good-quality red wine vinegar

  ⅓ cup extra virgin olive oil

  ⅓ cup freshly grated parmesan

  freshly ground black pepper to taste

Combine all ingredients in the bottom of a large salad bowl, whisk to combine, taste for seasoning, adjust if necessary, and reserve.

FOR THE PARMESAN GARLIC CROUTONS:

  olive oil cooking spray

  1 baguette cut into about 20 one-inch slices

  1 clove peeled garlic

  2 tablespoons shredded Parmesan cheese

STEPS:

1. Preheat the oven to 500 degrees.

2. Spray a cookie sheet with the olive oil cooking spray. Spread out the bread slices in one layer and spray them lightly, too.

3. Place in the oven. Allow to brown about two minutes and remove and rub the garlic clove on the browned side of the bread.

4. Turn the slices over and spray lightly with the cooking spray. Place them in the oven to brown about another two to three minute. Remove and sprinkle with the Parmesan cheese and place back in the oven to melt the cheese. Remove and reserve.

FOR THE SALAD:

1 large head of romaine lettuce

STEPS:

1. Wash and dry the leaves of lettuce and tear into bite-size pieces. You should have approximately six very large handfuls.

2. Place in the salad bowl atop the dressing, add croutons, toss, and serve immediately.

Egg-White Protein and Gout

High consumption of meat protein can contribute to the onset of gout. In contrast, the protein contained in dairy products can help keep gout at bay or at least limit its effects. The best and purist of dairy proteins comes from the white of the egg.

White Hearts Salad

Serves four to six

In our version of egg salad, you won't miss the yolks. This salad offers a nice blend of tart and creamy. It is terrific on its own or spread on pumpernickel bread. If you prefer it less tart, omit the vinegar. If you are a curry fan, adding two teaspoons of curry powder and one tablespoon mango chutney will turn this salad a beautiful color and make it more flavorful.

INGREDIENTS:

> 16 egg whites, hard-cooked and diced
> ⅓ cup egg white mayonnaise (see recipe below)
> 3 stalks hearts of palm (from a can) diced to yield ½ cup
> ¼ small white onion, minced
> 1 stalk celery heart, diced to yield ½ cup
> 1 tablespoon chopped chervil
> salt and pepper
> 1 teaspoon champagne vinegar (optional)
> 2 heads endive, cleaned, leaves separated

FOR THE EGG-WHITE MAYONNAISE:

> 1 tablespoon champagne vinegar
> ¼ cup egg whites, such as Egg Beaters
> ¼ teaspoon dry mustard
> 1 cup safflower or canola oil
> salt and pepper to taste

TO MAKE THE MAYONNAISE: *Makes 1 cup*

1. In the food processor combine the vinegar, egg whites, and dry mustard. Pulse to combine for ten to twenty seconds.

2. With processor running, slowly pour in oil through the feed tube. You will hear a sound when mixture starts to emulsify slurping, continue to process until all the oil is incorporated about one minute.

3. Season to taste with salt and pepper.

To make the white heart salad:

1. Hard-boil the eggs. Cool, peel, and discard the yolks. Alternatively, poach the egg whites for ten minutes, or until firm, in the egg poacher. Dice egg whites and reserve in a medium mixing bowl.

2. Add a third of a cup of mayonnaise, hearts of palm, onion, celery hearts, chopped chervil, and mix. Season with salt and pepper (and optional vinegar) to taste.

3. Stuff endive leaves with egg white salad and garnish plate with a few sprigs of chervil.

4. Serve with a dense dark bread, such as pumpernickel.

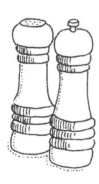

COOKING TIP

To fix a "broken" or oily mayonnaise start over in a clean processor, add one teaspoon prepared mustard, and with processor running slowly pour "broken" mayonnaise back into the container and process thirty seconds or so.

Warm Lentil Salad
with Crispy Fried Egg Whites

Serves six to eight

Lentils paired with egg whites make this salad as nutritionally complete as it is tasty. Leftover lentil salad (if there is any) can be used to stuff a tomato or as a side dish with grilled fish the next day. Try to find the tiny French green lentils called lentils de Puy for this dish. If you can't find them, you can substitute red lentils or the common brown ones.

INGREDIENTS:

- 1 teaspoon olive oil
- 3 shallots, minced
- 1 pound lentils de Puy (French lentils can be found in the gourmet store), rinsed and picked over for small stones
- 1 bouquet garni (two four-inch celery sticks stuffed with two bay leaves and parsley leaves and tied together with string)
- cooking spray
- 12 egg whites

MUSTARD VINAIGRETTE:

- 2 tablespoons Dijon mustard
- 1 teaspoon dried mustard
- 2 tablespoons wine vinegar
- 4 tablespoons olive oil
- 2 tablespoons fresh thyme leaves
- salt and pepper to taste

FOR THE GARNISH:

- 1 large tomato, chopped
- 2 tablespoons chives

STEPS:

1. In a medium saucepan, heat the olive oil over medium heat and sauté the shallot for three to five minutes until translucent. Add the lentils and bouquet garni and cover with water. Bring to a boil, reduce the heat, and simmer uncovered for thirty minutes or until the lentils become tender. Remove from the heat, drain the water, and remove the bouquet garni and discard. Reserve the lentils and cover to keep warm.

2. Combine the vinaigrette ingredients in a large bowl and whisk together. Add the lentils and toss to coat. Taste for seasoning.

3. Heat a large nonstick skillet over high heat and spray with the cooking spray. Pour in the egg whites and fry them five minutes until edges become brown and crispy. Turn the pancake over with a spatula and cook another three to five minutes until crispy. Remove from skillet and cut into six wedges.

4. Scoop about one cup of the warm lentils onto the individual serving plate. Place the egg white wedge on top, sprinkle with chopped tomato and chives, and serve.

Red and White Salad

Serves six to eight

This is a great salad to take along on a picnic or as a potluck salad. Using canned beans and beets in this recipe makes this very simple and easy to prepare, although you could easily substitute fresh ingredients if you are feeling ambitious. Either way, you will entertain your guests with an interesting and satisfying side salad that can be made into a meal with the addition of a crusty garlic bread or other accompaniment.

INGREDIENTS:

> 1 can (15.5 ounces) garbanzo beans, rinsed and drained
> or 1½ cups cooked beans
> 1 can (15.5 ounces) kidney beans or pink beans,
> or 1½ cups cooked beans
> 1 can (15 ounces) diced beets, drained, or 4 medium beets,
> cooked and diced
> 8 egg whites, hard-cooked, diced
> ½ red onion, minced

SWEET AND SOUR VINAIGRETTE:

> 2 tablespoons cider vinegar
> 1 tablespoon honey
> 3 tablespoons canola oil
> 1 orange, zested and juiced
> 1 tablespoon chopped fresh dill
> salt and pepper to taste

STEPS:

1. Place the beans, beets, egg whites, and onion in a large mixing bowl and toss to combine.

2. In a small bowl, whisk the vinaigrette ingredients to combine, pour over beans and refrigerate at least two hours before serving. Before serving, toss again, and taste for seasoning.

Chapter 7
Sandwiches

A sandwich is the best way to simplify a great meal.

—Attributed to the Earl of Sandwich

With the advent of low-carb bread products, sandwiches—always a favorite choice for lunch—have been miraculously resurrected as a healthy choice for a fast and satisfying lunch. We've invented some tasty ways to make egg whites a centerpiece in some delicious "new age" sandwiches. Feel free to experiment with new breads, buns, pita pockets, tortillas, and more. And if you have leftovers from your White Hearts Salad or another egg white recipe you've tried in the salad or dinner section, you might try them as fine filler for sandwich fare. And, of course, there is still nothing like the soup-and-sandwich combination. We've given you many choices to make this immortal standard work for you.

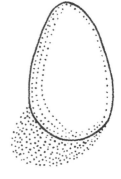

Crispy Whites and Veggie Wrap

Serves eight

Have you seen broccoli slaw in the produce section of the supermarket? It's the shredded stems of the broccoli plant, and it is delicious. If you can't find it, you can certainly use your own broccoli stems and peel and shred them in a food processor. But if you can find it in the bag—go for it.

INGREDIENTS:

> cooking spray
> 20 egg whites
> 2 teaspoons Goya seasoning mix or substitute
> 2 cups shredded broccoli stems
> 2 cups tomato salsa
> 12 ounces Monterey Jack (or other mild flavored cheese), shredded
> 4 whole wheat wraps (twelve inches in diameter)

STEPS:

1. Heat a large, nonstick skillet over medium heat. Spray with cooking spray. Pour five egg whites into skillet and allow to cook around the edges; move the edges with the spatula and allow the uncooked egg white to flow to the bottom.

2. Sprinkle on the seasoning mix and half a cup of shredded broccoli. Cook five minutes until browned and almost set. Flip over and cook another five minutes until cooked through. Repeat with the remaining ingredients to make four pancakes altogether.

3. Prepare each wrap by spreading it with a quarter cup salsa and three ounces of the shredded cheese each. Place the veggie pancake on top, fold in the sides, and roll up tightly.

4. Cut each wrap in half and serve immediately with the additional salsa on the side.

Danish Smoked Trout
and Egg White Sandwich

Makes six lunch servings

These open-faced sandwiches are as beautiful to look at as they are delicious to eat. They make for a truly festive brunch and also work well as hors d'oeuvres. If you are not a smoked fish fan, try using a smoked meat, like sausage, bacon, or turkey instead of the fish.

INGREDIENTS:

> 12 slices pumpernickel bread or other dense dark bread, crusts removed
>
> 2 tablespoons unsalted butter or butter substitute, softened
>
> ½ cup watercress leaves
>
> 8 ounces smoked trout or other smoked fish
>
> 24 egg whites, hard-cooked, cut into strips
>
> ½ red onion, sliced paper-thin
>
> 3 teaspoons capers

STEPS:

1. Butter the bread slices and layer on the ingredients in the order listed above, equally divided among the bread slices.

2. Cut on the diagonal into two triangular shapes and serve four pieces per guest. If you are using this recipe as an hors d'oeuvre, cut each bread slice into four pieces and serve on a large serving platter.

Fried Egg White Sandwiches

Just the other day, we overheard a young woman in our local deli ordering "egg whites and ham on rye toast" for lunch. We were overjoyed to find that our favorite protein is being eaten as a healthy, fast-food alternative. So fry up some egg whites and make them a part of your favorite sandwiches. Here are just some of the limitless possibilities:

- Grilled (low-fat) cheese and egg white sandwiches

- Grilled pepper and egg white sandwiches

- Ham and egg white sandwiches

- Tomato and egg white sandwiches

- Peanut butter and egg white sandwiches

- Cucumber, sprouts, and egg white sandwiches

- Avocado, tomato, and egg white sandwiches

- Turkey bacon, (low-fat) cheese, and egg white sandwiches

The list goes on, depending on your tastes and preferences.

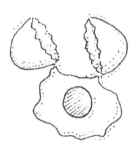

French Toast Sandwiches

Makes six sandwiches

This is a great recipe for your George Foreman grill, griddle, or skillet. The sandwiches are especially good served with condiments such as a good grainy mustard, mango chutney, cranberry relish, herbed mayonnaise, or sun-dried tomato pesto. Cut into bite-sized servings, they make a fantastic hors d'oeuvre.

INGREDIENTS:

> 8 egg whites
> ¾ cup low-fat milk
> a pinch of nutmeg
> salt and pinch of freshly ground black pepper
> 1 good whole wheat loaf of bread, sliced into 12 slices
> ½ pound Black Forest ham
> ½ pound Gruyère or Jarlsberg cheese
> 1 tablespoon fresh thyme leaves
> 1 bunch watercress (for garnish), trimmed

STEPS:

1. Heat your George Foreman grill, or another stovetop grill, or set aside a large nonstick skillet.

2. Beat egg whites with milk, nutmeg, and salt and pepper in a medium-size bowl.

3. To assemble sandwiches with ham and cheese, you will need about three thin slices of ham (1½ ounces per sandwich) and about 1¼ ounce cheese or two thin slices.

4. Dip the sandwiches in egg mixture briefly, turning once until bread is soaked through; squeeze out excess egg mixture from sandwich.

5. Grill sandwich for five to seven minutes until golden-brown or heat a skillet/griddle over medium heat and grill sandwich four minutes per side until golden-brown and cheese has melted.

6. Serve immediately on a plate garnished with watercress and the condiment of your choice.

TRY THESE OTHER COMBINATIONS
FOR YOUR SANDWICH FILLINGS:

• 1½ ounces goat cheese per sandwich, two or three fresh figs sliced thin, and several thin slices prosciuitto

• Sautéed pear and brie—half a pear sliced thin and 1½ ounces brie per sandwich

• Peanut butter and banana—half a banana and two or three teaspoons crunchy peanut butter

Chapter 8
Small, White
Bites and Snacks

A little in one's own pocket is better than
much in another man's purse. 'Tis good to
keep a nest egg. Every little makes a nickle.
—Miguel de Cervantes

E ven a little bit or bite can be a great thing. Here are
some ideas that may brighten an evening's dinner
party or, perhaps, just be treats for you and yours. And if
you do give a party and there are leftovers, these all are
easily saved for a day or two. Enjoy!

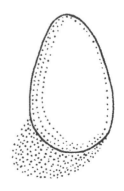

Asparagus and Egg White Nori Rolls

Makes thirty-six pieces

We bring these to potluck parties because they are so pretty when arranged on a silver or mirrored tray but also are the perfect finger food, which makes them a star at any buffet. The secret is they're simple and quick to make once you get the hang of rolling sushi on a bamboo mat. We have even taught children the art of rolling sushi. The bamboo rolling mats are sold in the Asian section of most grocery stores. Serve these with pickled ginger and soy dipping sauce.

INGREDIENTS:

> 2 cups sushi rice
>
> 4 cups water
>
> 2 tablespoons seasoned rice vinegar
>
> pinch of sea salt
>
> 6 sheets nori
>
> 6 asparagus stalks, trimmed and steamed

FOR THE PANCAKES:

> 8 egg whites
>
> 1 tablespoon mirin (Japanese sweet cooking wine) or sherry
>
> 1 tablespoon soy sauce
>
> 1 teaspoon sesame oil
>
> 1 whole scallion, trimmed and sliced into thin rounds
>
> cooking spray

STEPS:

1. Place rice in a large bowl and wash with cold running water in the sink for ten minutes. Drain rice in a large colander and let dry twenty minutes.

2. Place washed rice and water into a pot and bring to a boil. Reduce heat and cover. Cook fifteen minutes or until all the water has been absorbed. Turn off heat and allow to sit for ten minutes.

3. Remove rice from the pot and spread out onto a large pan. Pour the seasoned rice vinegar over the rice and mix carefully with a flat wooden paddle or flat wooden spoon so as not to break the grains of rice. Allow rice to cool.

4. To start on the pancakes, mix the egg whites in a small bowl with the soy sauce, the mirin, sesame oil, and scallions. Set aside.

5. Heat a small (six-inch) nonstick skillet over medium heat and spray with cooking spray. Pour three tablespoons egg mixture into skillet and cook one minute. When top begins to set, flip over using chopsticks or a small spatula. Cook another thirty seconds. Remove to a plate to cool and reserve. Repeat with the rest of the egg mixture. You should have six pancakes.

6. Place a sheet of nori, shiny side down, on top of the bamboo roller. Place approximately ⅔ cup of the cooked rice onto the nori, spreading it evenly over the entire surface, leaving a half-inch border at the top. Place a spear of asparagus lengthwise and a whole pancake rolled up on top of the rice.

7. Begin rolling, lifting up the edge of the mat closest to you, and rolling it away from you, pressing down evenly on the bamboo as you roll. At the top wipe a few drops of water across the exposed edge of nori and finish rolling to seal it. Let the roll rest for ten minutes before slicing. Repeat with the remaining ingredients.

8. Cut each roll into six equal pieces using a long slicing knife. Arrange the rolls on serving platters and serve.

French Eggs

While it is customary to throw rice at the bride and groom in many countries, brides in France break an egg on the threshold of their new home for luck and good health.

Bacon, Tomato, and Egg White-Stuffed Mushrooms

Makes about sixteen stuffed mushrooms

Stuffed mushrooms offer yet another tasty use of the endlessly versatile egg white..
Serve these as a snack, a brunch item, or even as light lunch accompanied by a
green salad or one of our egg white salads.

INGREDIENTS:

> cooking spray
>
> 1¼ pounds white mushrooms (about 16 medium mushrooms)
>
> 6 slices turkey bacon, cooked crisp and crumbled
>
> 2 plum tomatoes, seeded and finely diced
>
> 4 egg whites, hard-cooked and finely minced
>
> ½ cup finely shredded Parmesan or Romano cheese
>
> ¼ teaspoon freshly ground black pepper

STEPS:

1. Preheat the oven to 400 degrees. Spray a baking tray with the cooking spray.

2. Wipe the mushrooms with a damp cloth to clean. Remove stems and discard.

3. Combine the bacon bits, tomatoes, egg whites, and cheese and season with the
   black pepper.

4. Equally divide the stuffing mixture between the mushrooms and stuff them. Place
   the mushrooms on the baking tray and spray them lightly with the cooking spray.

5. Bake fifteen minutes.

The Hard-Working Hen

*It takes a hen approximately twenty-four hours
to lay one egg. As they usually lay an egg a day,
the diligent hen is at work seven days a week.*

Stuffed Cherry Tomatoes

Makes fourteen tomatoes

This tasty little variation on the tried-and-true stuffed cherry tomato is perfect at a potluck party, picnic, or as easy-to-eat hors d'oeuvres, and it is a good conversation starter on how to enjoy scrumptious appetizers in a healthy form. People always want more. You could also use the stuffing mixture to stuff larger beefsteak tomatoes as a light lunch or side.

INGREDIENTS:

> 14 cherry tomatoes
> 4 tablespoons diced low-fat fresh mozzarella cheese (or feta cheese)
> 1 teaspoon olive oil
> 1 teaspoon balsamic vinegar
> 1 tablespoon fresh thyme leaves or basil leaves, minced
> 4 egg whites, hard-cooked and minced
> salt and pepper to taste

STEPS:

1. Cut the tops from the cherry tomatoes, scoop out the pulp and seeds and discard.

2. In a small bowl, combine the cheese with the olive oil, vinegar, thyme, egg whites, and salt and pepper.

3. Place one heaping teaspoonful into each cherry tomato. Place on a serving platter, garnish with fresh thyme sprigs, and serve.

Did you know that one ostrich egg is equivalent to twenty-two chicken eggs? This means that all you need to make an omelet for your Sunday brunch guests is one ostrich egg, if you can find it.

New Potatoes with Caviar and Egg White

Makes six to eight servings

It's best to use the little shooter marble-sized potatoes for this recipe. If you can't find those, use half of a small red potato. Just remember to make them bite-size so that they're not messy to eat, and can be consumed in one bite.

INGREDIENTS:

> 12–14 baby new potatoes (about one inch in diameter)
> ¼ cup non-fat sour cream
> 2 egg whites, hard cooked and minced
> 2 tablespoons black caviar or red salmon caviar
> 1 bunch fresh dill

STEPS:

1. Place washed potatoes in a medium saucepan and cover with cold water. Add one teaspoon salt and bring to a boil. Cook for eight to ten minutes until just tender when pierced with the tip of a knife. Remove from the heat, drain in a colander, and let cool.

2. When cool, using a small melon baller or small-tipped spoon, remove the top of the potato. Slice a small piece from bottom of potato to allow it to stand up on its own.

3. Spoon on about half a teaspoon of sour cream, top with minced egg whites, and garnish with the caviar.

4. On a serving platter, spread the dill fronds around, arrange the potatoes on top, and serve.

Un-deviled Eggs

Makes twelve egg-white halves

Remember deviled eggs, that fabulous 1950s food that was present at every cocktail party and family gathering? These un-deviled eggs will remind you of those but are so much healthier and tastier. Hard-cooked egg whites make the best vessels for these various fillings. Think of using these instead of crackers for your favorite soft cheeses, vegetable spreads, or tapenades, or try the fillings below.

INGREDIENTS:

> 6 raw eggs in their shells
> 6 ounces low-fat cream cheese
> 1 teaspoon curry powder
> 2 tablespoons mango chutney
> cilantro leaves for garnish

STEPS:

1. Place the eggs in a saucepan with cold water to cover, place over medium heat, and bring to a boil. Immediately remove from the heat and cover pan. Let sit for ten minutes, then drain and run cold water over them immediately, cracking the shell slightly. Let sit in the cold water until cool to the touch. Drain water and roll eggs around to crack the shell all over, then peel. Cut in half lengthwise and discard that pesky yolk.

2. Divide the stuffing mixture (choose from above) equally between the egg-white halves and stuff them. Top each with the appropriate garnish and skewer with a toothpick lengthwise and serve.

Variation: Use this filling for your egg white shells instead:
- 3 teaspoons prepared sun-dried tomato pesto or relish
- 6 ounces feta cheese
- 2 sun-dried tomatoes, sliced into thin slivers for garnish

Five-Spice Un-deviled
Eggs with Shrimp

Makes 12 egg white halves

Here's a different version of an un-deviled egg—one in which the egg white becomes marbleized and takes on a Chinese flavor as it cooks. These make excellent companions on the hors d'oeuvres tray with the Asparagus and Egg White Nori Rolls (on page 00). If you are serving these on a tray, skewer each one lengthwise with a long, frilled toothpick so they are easier to pick up.

INGREDIENTS:

> 6 raw eggs in their shells
> ½ cup soy sauce
> 3 black tea bags
> 5 star anise pods
> 1 tablespoon five-spice powder
> 1 teaspoon sesame oil
> 16 jumbo shrimp, finely minced
> 3 tablespoons cabbage, finely minced
> 1 tablespoon scallion, sliced paper-thin
> 2 teaspoons soy sauce mixed with 1 teaspoon cornstarch
> ¼ teaspoon hot pepper flakes (or to taste)
> 6 teaspoons sesame seeds

STEPS:

1. Place raw eggs in a large saucepan. Cover with two cups cold water, soy sauce, tea bags, star anise pods, and spice powder. Bring to a boil and then remove from the heat and immediately cover the pan. Let sit for ten minutes.

2. Remove the cover, remove the eggs, and crack the shells all around with the back of a spoon. Place the eggs back in the liquid and refrigerate for at least four hours.

3. Remove the eggs and discard liquid. Peel the eggs, cut in half lengthwise, and discard the yolks. Refrigerate the egg whites until you are ready to stuff them.

4. Heat the sesame oil in a medium skillet over medium heat. Add the shrimp and stir-fry two minutes. Add the cabbage, scallion, soy-cornstarch mixture, and hot pepper flakes. Cook another one to two minutes until the shrimp turns pink and the mixture thickens a bit. Remove from the heat and allow to cool somewhat.

5. Stuff the egg whites with the shrimp mixture and sprinkle sesame seeds over each egg white half. Skewer with a toothpick and serve.

Chapter 9

Main Course
Egg Whites

The codfish lays ten thousand eggs,
The homely hen lays one.
The codfish never cackles
To tell you what she's done.
And so we scorn the codfish,
While the humble hen we prize,
Which only goes to show you
That it pays to advertise.
—Anonymous

You might doubt the viability of egg whites in or as a main course, but egg whites find their place in dinner recipes as elegantly and as easily as they do in all other meals. We've paired egg whites with everything from chili, to fish dishes, to pasta carbonara with delicious results. These dinners are richly flavored, satisfying, and easy to make. You can rest assured that you are always getting protein of the highest order and lowest fat content.

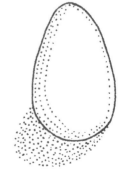

Ham, Pea, and Egg White Risotto

Serves four

This risotto has a fresh spring taste with its fresh peas and hint of mint. We use leftover baked ham, but you can substitute chopped white meat chicken, turkey, or whatever suits your fancy. Pair this with a mixed lettuce salad and you have a delicious meal.

INGREDIENTS:

4 cups chicken stock

1 cup white wine

2 teaspoons olive oil

2 shallots, minced

1½ cups arborio rice

1 cup chopped ham

1 cup fresh peas, cooked

4 egg whites, hard-cooked, diced

¼ cup freshly grated Parmesan cheese

freshly ground black pepper to taste

4 tablespoons chopped fresh mint (or parsley) for garnish

STEPS:

1. In a medium saucepan, combine the chicken stock and the wine and bring to a boil. Reduce heat and keep broth simmering.

2. In a heavy-bottomed saucepan or Dutch oven, place the olive oil and shallots and sauté for three to five minutes over medium heat until translucent. Add the rice and sauté one to two minutes more until grains are opaque and pearly. Add half a cup of hot broth and stir with a wooden spoon until it has been absorbed before adding more. Repeat with all the broth; this should take twenty to twenty-five minutes. Add the ham, peas, egg whites, and Parmesan cheese and stir to combine. Season to taste with the freshly ground black pepper. Sprinkle with the chopped mint or parsley and serve.

Spaghetti Pie

Serves six

If you're tired of the same old spaghetti dinners, try this fun twist on an old favorite. You'll enjoy the fact that's it's a make-ahead dish that can be popped into the oven and ready to serve in twenty minutes. It's also low-fat and healthy to boot.

INGREDIENTS:

cooking spray

4 cups cooked spaghetti (half a pound), use a combination of whole wheat and regular pasta

1 tablespoon olive oil

½ cup low-fat ricotta cheese

⅓ cup freshly grated Parmesan cheese

2 egg whites

1½ cups of your favorite marinara sauce

freshly ground black pepper to taste

8 ounces fresh mozzarella, low-fat mozzarella, or Fontina cheese, shredded

½ cup torn basil leaves for garnish

STEPS:

1. Preheat the oven to 350 degrees. Spray a light coating of the cooking spray on a ten-inch pie pan.

2. Place the cooked spaghetti in a large bowl, and toss with the olive oil.

3. In a small bowl, combine the ricotta cheese, Parmesan, egg whites, and sauce. Season with the black pepper.

4. Combine the marinara mixture with the spaghetti and toss to coat.

5. Spoon pasta into the prepared pie plate and top with the shredded mozzarella.

6. Place in oven and bake twenty to twenty-five minutes. Remove from the oven, garnish with the basil leaves, cut into six wedges, and serve.

Rigatoni with Bacon, Egg White, and Parmesan

Serves six

This version of spaghetti carbonara contains a lot less fat and calories than the original but is just as satisfying and simple to make, using only one pot, one skillet, and one serving bowl.

INGREDIENTS:

    4 slices good quality bacon or turkey bacon
    1 clove garlic, minced
    1 shallot, minced
    ½ cup dry white wine or an Italian beer
    ¾ pound dried rigatoni
    3 egg whites
    ⅓ cup freshly grated Parmesan cheese
    freshly ground black pepper to taste
    1 tablespoon grated lemon zest
    2 tablespoons chopped fresh thyme or parsley

STEPS:

1. Place the bacon in a medium skillet and cook over medium heat until crisp, five to seven minutes turning over once. Remove bacon, drain on paper towels, and crumble into bite-sized pieces and reserve.

2. Pour off all but one tablespoon of the bacon fat from the skillet and add the garlic and shallot. Sauté for three to five minutes over medium heat until slightly browned.

3. Add the white wine (or the beer) to deglaze the skillet and reduce the liquid until two to three tablespoons remain. Add crumbled bacon back to the skillet and reserve off the heat.

4. In the meantime, bring a large pot of water to a boil for the rigatoni and cook according to package instructions.

5. Whisk the egg whites with the Parmesan in a medium bowl and season to taste with lots of freshly ground black pepper.

5. Drain pasta and add back to the skillet immediately along with the egg and cheese mixture.

6. Add the zest and fold the mixture together quickly. Spoon into the serving bowl, garnish with the chopped thyme (or parsley), and serve.

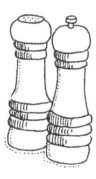

COOKING TIP

Remember the key here is timing. You need to have all your ingredients ready before you start making this dish. It is crucial that the hot pasta be mixed with the egg and cheese mixture before it has a chance to cool, "cooking" the egg sauce from the heat of the pasta.

INGREDIENTS, CENTER STAGE

Use only the best quality ingredients you can find and freshly grate the Parmesan cheese and the black pepper for this dish. The simpler the dish, the more important it is not to scrimp on your ingredients, as each one is performing center stage.

Broccoli, No Yolk Casserole

Serves eight

This recipe was inspired by one created by Lana of Lana's Whites see page 16. It is easy to make and store overnight and impossible to resist. It's also endlessly versatile; check out the varieties following the recipe. The noodles we like to use are made with just egg white, no yolk, hence, the name.

INGREDIENTS:

cooking spray
1 teaspoon olive oil
1 medium onion, diced
12 ounces No-Yolk noodles (an egg white noodle product sold in the dried pasta section of the market)
2 cups broccoli florets
8 egg whites
1 cup fat-free sour cream
¼ cup fat-free condensed milk
½ cup shredded low-fat mozzarella
½ cup shredded low-fat cheddar
3 ounces sun-dried tomatoes, minced
¼ cup pine nuts
salt and freshly ground black pepper

STEPS:

1. Preheat oven to 350 degrees. Spray a three- to four-quart baking dish with cooking spray.

2. In a large skillet, add olive oil and onions and sauté four to five minutes over medium heat until it turns translucent. Remove from the heat and reserve.

3. In a large pot bring water to boil and cook noodles five minutes. Add broccoli florets and cook another five minutes; drain and reserve.

4. In a large mixing bowl, combine the cooked noodles and broccoli with the egg

whites, sour cream, milk, cheeses, sun-dried tomatoes, pine nuts, and salt and pepper, and stir thoroughly.

5. Spoon the mixture into the baking dish. Cover with aluminum foil and bake twenty-five minutes. Serve immediately.

Try using these combinations of cooked ingredients instead of the ones listed above:

- Chickpeas and roasted red peppers

- Sausage, broccoli rabe, and hot peppers

- Roasted eggplant, zucchini, and tomato

- Cauliflower, roasted garlic, oil-cured olives, and raisins

- Scallops, tarragon, and peas

Black and White Chili

Serves six to eight

This dish is fast and easy to prepare—and pretty too! A good vegetarian dish for a crowd, this can be made days ahead, except for the egg whites, and then heated just before serving. As a matter of fact, this is better if it is made in advance and the flavors have a chance to develop. This is great served with the Zucchini Corn Bread (on page 60).

Fresh black beans provide great flavor, but never salt the water while cooking the beans as it will make the skins tough. Canned black beans are a great time saver and are eminently interchangeable here.

INGREDIENTS:

2½ cups black beans (a 16-ounce package) or 4 cans Goya black
   beans, rinsed and drained
4 tablespoons olive oil
2 large onions, diced
2 green peppers, diced
1 or 2 (to taste) jalapeno peppers, seeds and white ribs removed,
   minced
4 teaspoons chili powder
2 teaspoons cumin powder
2 teapoons cocoa powder
1 teaspoon dried coriander
1 teaspoon dried oregano
½ teaspoon dried thyme
1 tablespoon salt, or to taste
1 yellow summer squash, diced
2 cups white corn kernels
1 28-ounce can chopped tomatoes
1 6-ounce can tomato paste
2 chipotle peppers, diced, and two tablespoons adobo sauce from
   canned chipotle in adobo sauce (Goya brand or La Morena) (optional)
4 hard-cooked egg whites, diced, to yield 1 ½ cups

Garnish with shredded Monterey jack cheese, chopped fresh cilantro, and non-fat sour cream

STEPS:

1. Soak the dried beans in water overnight to cover by two inches. Drain. Place beans in large pot, cover with water, and cook over medium heat about an hour and a half until tender. Skim off foam, but don't stir.

2. In a large pot or Dutch oven, add the olive oil and onions and sauté about five minutes over medium heat until they begin to turn translucent. Add the green and jalapeno peppers and sauté another minute. Add powdered spices and salt and sauté until spices release their fragrance, about two or three minutes.

3. Add rest of ingredients except egg whites and stir; add a quarter- to a half-cup of water if mixture looks too dry. Cover and cook over medium heat for fifteen to twenty minutes. Add egg whites and taste for seasoning. Remove from heat and serve with the garnishes passed alongside.

Wine and Egg-White Fare

Egg-white dishes tend to coat the palate and teeth, posing an impediment if you wish to enjoy a fine wine with your meal. Therefore, it is best to serve them with uncomplicated varieties like rosés, sparkling wines, and fino sherries.

Red Bean and Egg White Enchiladas

Serves four to six

These enchiladas are made with egg white pancakes instead of the traditional tortillas and make a delicious vegetarian dish. Served as a casserole topped with a homemade tomatillo (green husked tomato) salsa, these are easy to make, gorgeous to present, and even more fun to eat. Try making this easy fresh salsa when you tire of the bottled kind. To make the salsa, place all of the ingredients in the bowl of a food processor or blender and process until smooth. Taste for seasoning and set aside.

INGREDIENTS:

> cooking spray
> 12 egg whites, lightly beaten
> 1 medium onion, minced, divided
> 2 10.5-ounce cans enchilada sauce
> 4 chipotle peppers in adobo sauce from a four-ounce can of chipotole peppers in adobo sauce (Goya brand or La Morena) (optional)
> 1 clove garlic, minced
> 2 10.5-ounce cans pinto beans, drained and rinsed
> 8 ounces Monterey Jack cheese, shredded

FOR THE SALSA:

> cooking spray
> 2 garlic cloves, peeled
> 2 pounds plum tomatoes, halved
> 5 fresh serrano chilies
> 2 tablespoons chopped onion
> 2 tablespoons olive oil
> salt to taste

STEPS:

1. Preheat oven to 350 degrees. Spray a ten-inch nonstick skillet with cooking spray. Over medium heat, pour in a third of a cup of egg whites.

2. Cook one to two minutes until top is set; turn over and cook another two minutes more. Reserve and repeat with remaining egg whites, spraying the skillet as necessary with the cooking spray to get eight pancakes.

3. Spray a large skillet with cooking spray, add one half of the minced onion and sauté five to seven minutes over medium heat until it turns translucent. Add the enchilada sauce, four chipotle peppers, and the adobo sauce from the can. Reduce the heat to low and cook for ten minutes. Remove from the heat and allow to cool. Transfer to a blender or use a wand blender to purée the sauce until smooth.

4. Spray another large skillet with cooking spray, add the other half of the minced onion and sauté five to seven minutes over medium heat until it turns translucent. Add the drained beans, stir and cook another two minutes. Remove from heat and reserve.

5. In a ten- by thirteen-inch baking dish, spread a layer of the enchilada sauce on the bottom, lay an egg white pancake on top of the sauce and top it with some of the bean mixture and shredded cheese mixture. Roll up into a log. Repeat with remaining pancakes. Pour enchilada sauce over rolled pancakes and top with remaining shredded cheese.

6. Bake fifteen to twenty minutes until cheese has melted and enchiladas are heated through. Remove from the oven.

7. Spread some salsa on top and serve. Alternately, pass the salsa alongside the dish and let guests help themselves.

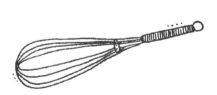

Fried Flounder on a
Bed of Sautéed Spinach

Serves six

The panko called for in this recipe is a Japanese large breadcrumb product, which produces a really crispy coating and can be found in specialty or Asian markets. If you can't find the spinach and chive panko breadcrumbs, you can use any flavored breadcrumbs for this recipe. You can also add chopped chives to a plain variety of breadcrumbs.

INGREDIENTS:

> 3 egg whites, lighten beaten
> 1 cup spinach and chive panko (Japanese) breadcrumbs
> 6 6-ounce flounder fillets
> cooking spray
> 1½ pounds fresh baby spinach, washed and dried
> ½ lemon, juiced
> 1 tablespoon grated lemon zest
> salt and freshly ground black pepper to taste

STEPS:

1. Put the beaten egg whites in a medium shallow bowl. On a flat plate, lay out the breadcrumbs. Dip each fillet into the egg white and then into the breadcrumbs, patting them to help them adhere to the fish. Set aside.

2. Heat a large nonstick skillet over high heat and spray with cooking spray. Add the spinach leaves and sauté two minutes until just wilted; add lemon juice, zest, and salt and pepper to taste. Remove from the heat and cover to keep warm.

3. Spray a large nonstick skillet with the cooking spray and add the fish fillets in a single layer, being careful not to crowd the pan. Sauté the fish fillets three to four minutes over medium heat-high heat; turn over and sauté on the other side another three to five minutes until nicely browned and cooked through.

4. To serve, place equal amounts of the spinach on six serving plates, top each with a flounder fillet and serve.

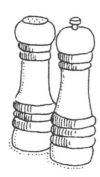

COOKING TIP

Our foolproof method for dipping and frying goes like this: one hand is your "dry" hand and the other is your "wet" hand. Using your "wet" or left hand dip the food into the liquid mixture (egg or milk), remove the food with the "wet" hand and drop it into the dry mixture (never touching the dry mix with that hand). Use your "dry" hand to coat the food and place on the cooking surface. Repeat with the remaining food items to be breaded.

Salmon Cakes with Tarragon Sauce

Makes eight cakes, about four servings

Go ahead and use canned salmon for this dish, however, if you prefer fresh salmon and can find it easily, manage the expense, and have the time to prepare it, these salmon cakes will be even more delicious. It's a snap to mix up the ingredients and only a few minutes to cook them, making this an easy weekday meal for families. Our kids like to eat them as salmon burgers on a bun with lettuce, tomato, and mayonnaise. Try making them as hors d'oeuvres for your next party.

INGREDIENTS:

1 medium stalk celery , minced

½ small red onion, minced

½ small bunch parsley, stemmed and chopped finely

1 tablespoon dried mustard powder

¼ teaspoon paprika

1 tablespoon salt

1 teaspoon black pepper

1 cup panko (Japanese) breadcrumbs or regular breadcrumbs

2 tablespoons capers, drained

2 tablespoons good quality Dijon mustard

1 tablespoon lemon juice

3 egg whites

6 drops Tabasco (or to taste)

2 7.5-ounce cans salmon

FOR THE TARRAGON SAUCE:

½ cup non-fat yogurt

½ cup non-fat sour cream

grated zest of one lemon

1 tablespoon lemon juice

2 tablespoons chopped fresh tarragon

3 tablespoons chopped fresh chives

1 teaspoon dry mustard

salt and pepper to taste

Tabasco to taste

STEPS:

1. Make the sauce by combining all the ingredients in a small bowl. Taste and season to your liking. Refrigerate until use.

2. In a medium mixing bowl, combine all ingredients up to the salmon. Stir well. Add drained, flaked salmon (drain it in a colander over the sink and pick through it for small bones) and mix well.

3. Using a quarter-cup measure, scoop out a heaping cupful and form into a patty. Set aside on a cookie sheet. Refrigerate covered on a cookie sheet for at least one hour.

4. Heat a large, nonstick skillet over high heat. Spray with cooking spray. Reduce heat to medium and sauté four cakes at a time, four to five minutes per side, until nicely browned.

Greek Salt-Crusted Halibut

Serves six

This dish creates a spectacular table presentation. It puffs up high as it bakes (thanks to the egg whites) and you have to crack open the salt crust at the table. The ensuing aromas that escape are mouth-watering, always delivering oohs and aahs from the guests assembled.

INGREDIENTS:

> 3 to 4 pounds kosher salt
>
> 1 cup egg whites
>
> 1 cup water
>
> 15 grape leaves (from a 1-pound jar of brined leaves)
>
> 6 halibut fillets, about 6 to 8 ounces each,
>   or other firm white fish fillets
>
> 1 lemon, sliced paper-thin
>
> ½ bunch fresh oregano
>
> freshly ground black pepper

FOR THE OLIVE AND TOMATO SALSA:

> 18 Greek olives, pitted, and chopped
>
> 4 plum tomatoes, seeded, and chopped
>
> 1 tablespoon fresh oregano leaves, chopped
>
> 3 tablespoons olive oil
>
> ½ lemon, juiced
>
> freshly ground black pepper

STEPS:

1. Preheat oven to 400 degrees.

2. Combine the salsa ingredients in a medium mixing bowl, season with the black pepper, and reserve.

3. In a large bowl, combine salt, egg whites, and about one cup of the water to form a paste with a texture like sherbet.

4. Working quickly with half of the salt paste, spread a layer of paste three-quarters of an inch thick in a ten- by thirteen-inch baking dish. Place about seven to eight of the grape leaves on top of salt, completely covering it. Place fish fillets on top of the leaves, lay the lemon slices on top of the fish with three or four sprigs of the fresh oregano, and then sprinkle with freshly ground pepper. Completely cover the fish fillets with the remaining leaves and top with the remaining salt paste. Place three to four oregano sprigs on top of the salt crust for decorative purposes.

5. Bake for twenty to twenty-five minutes, or until a thermometer inserted into the thickest part of a fillet reads 130 degrees. Remove from the oven and bring to the table to serve. Break through the crust with a large serving fork, remove it, and discard. Place a fillet on a plate, leaving the grape leaves in the baking dish, and garnish with a few spoonfuls of the salsa.

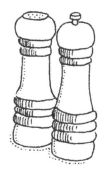

COOKING TIP

If you can't find grape leaves in the jar but have access to fresh ones, you can use them by blanching them in hot water first. You could also substitute blanched fresh Swiss chard or Napa cabbage leaves. The leaves will not be eaten but serve as protection for the fish fillets.

Grilled Asparagus and Tuna Rafts

Serves six

This is a great dish for summer entertaining. It can be cooked on an outdoor grill or an indoor stovetop one, and can be served room temperature or hot. Much of its preparation can be done in advance, such as making the roasted garlic sauce and skewering the "rafts." If you're grilling on the barbeque, fry the egg whites in a pan placed on top of the grill.

INGREDIENTS:

> 36 large asparagus spears
> olive oil cooking spray
> 6 tuna fillets, about 5 to 6 ounces each, one inch thick
> salt and pepper
> zest of 1 lemon
> cooking spray
> 12 egg whites
> 4 tablespoons chopped fresh chives (for garnish)

FOR THE ROASTED GARLIC SAUCE:

> 5 cloves garlic, roasted in the oven for 30 minutes, and peeled
> 1 tablespoon white wine vinegar
> 4 egg whites (pasteurized)
> ¼ teaspoon dry mustard
> 1 tablespoon chopped fresh tarragon leaves
> 1 cup olive oil
> salt and pepper to taste

STEPS:

1. To make the roasted garlic sauce: combine the garlic, vinegar, egg whites, dry mustard, and tarragon in a food processor. Pulse to combine for ten to twenty seconds. With the processor running, slowly pour in oil through the feed tube. You will hear a different sound when mixture starts to emulsify. Continue to

process until all the oil is incorporated, about one minute. Season to taste with salt and pepper. Reserve.

2. Using two bamboo skewers, form a raft with the asparagus by joining six of them together, alternating stem to tip. Spray the "rafts" with olive oil spray on both sides and set aside.

3. Rub the tuna fillets with a light coating of olive oil spray and salt and pepper. Grill them over a medium-hot grill, five minutes per side for well-done tuna. Set aside and keep warm. Grill the asparagus rafts about five minutes per side until lightly browned, remove from the heat, and sprinkle them with the lemon zest.

4. In a six-inch non-stick skillet over medium heat, spray with cooking spray and add two egg whites and cook until brown and crispy around the edges, about two to three minutes. Turn over and cook another one to two minutes until set. Remove from skillet and reserve. Repeat with the remaining egg whites, spraying with cooking spray as necessary.

5. Assemble the dish: place one raft on the plate, remove skewers, top with the grilled tuna, crispy fried egg white, and several spoonfuls of the roasted garlic sauce. Garnish with chopped chives and serve hot or room temperature.

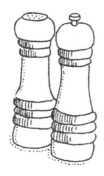

COOKING TIP

To assemble the asparagus rafts, skewer six pieces of asparagus together using two- to six-inch-long bamboo skewers (soaked in water for about twenty minutes first so they don't burn up). Skewering the asparagus together makes them easier to grill and the rafts make this dish that much more entertaining for your guests.

Oven-Baked Chicken Fingers

Serves eight

This recipe makes a lot of chicken fingers. Our kids like to eat them with lots of ketchup but try barbeque sauce, honey mustard, your favorite peanut sauce, or nothing but a little sea salt and fresh-squeezed lime juice. Beware, these go quickly!

INGREDIENTS:

> cooking spray
> 1 cup salted dry-roasted peanuts or cashews
> ½ cup wheat germ
> ½ cup unseasoned breadcrumbs or Japanese panko breadcrumbs
> 5 egg whites
> 1 teaspoon salt
> ½ teaspoon freshly ground black pepper
> 2 pounds chicken tenders

STEPS:

1. Preheat oven to 350 degrees. Spray two cookie sheets with the cooking spray.

2. Place the peanuts in a food processor and process for thirty seconds until finely ground. Add the wheat germ and breadcrumbs and process another ten seconds to combine. Pour out onto a flat plate.

3. Lightly whisk the egg whites and season with the salt and pepper.

4. Using the wet/dry hand technique described on page 115, bread the chicken fingers and place them on the cookie sheets.

5. Bake twenty minutes, remove from the oven, turn them over, and bake another ten minutes or until crisp. Serve hot or cold, with a barbeque dipping sauce and honey mustard or peanut sauce, whatever you and your guests prefer.

COOKING TIP: A NOTE ON GARLIC

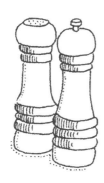

Roasted garlic has a lovely nutty flavor, milder than fresh garlic, and we both use it as often as possible. Keep a supply of roasted garlic on hand in the refrigerator.

To roast a head of garlic, first coat the head lightly with olive oil spray, then place it on a baking sheet in a 350-degree oven for thirty to forty minutes. Then remove the garlic, wrap in aluminum foil, and keep it in the refrigerator for about a week. Use it in recipes that call for fresh garlic such as salad dressings, sauces, and dips, or just simply spread it on hot crusty bread for a pungent bruschetta. The garlic will last you for days or weeks, depending on how much you love garlic.

Fried Red Tomatoes and Whites

Serves four to six

This makes a great and easy luncheon, but we also found it to be a tempting dinner entrée, especially when served with our Caesar salad with the egg white dressing (see page 80) and a crusty bread. Serve this and you will find your guests and family asking for more.

INGREDIENTS:

¼ cup finely ground yellow or white cornmeal
5 tablespoons freshly grated Parmesan cheese
¼ teaspoon salt and a pinch of freshly ground black pepper
2 large tomatoes, sliced into half-inch rounds (six slices)
cooking spray
1 pound fresh, rinsed and dried baby spinach leaves
½ cup evaporated skimmed milk
salt and pepper
pinch of freshly ground nutmeg
6 slices Canadian bacon or Canadian turkey bacon
12 egg whites

STEPS:

1. On a plate or shallow bowl, combine the cornmeal with two tablespoons of the Parmesan cheese and salt and pepper. Dredge the tomato slices on both sides and set aside.

2. Heat a large nonstick skillet and spray with cooking spray. Sauté tomato slices three to four minutes per side. Set aside and cover to keep warm.

3. In another large skillet over medium heat, combine the spinach and milk and cook for three to five minutes. Season with the remaining Parmesan, salt, pepper, and nutmeg. Reduce heat to low, place the Canadian bacon slices on top of the spinach, cover the skillet, and allow to heat through for five to seven minutes.

4. Poach the egg whites. Heat water in your egg poacher to boiling, spray egg containers with cooking spray, add two egg whites per container, cover, and

poach five to seven minutes until the whites are just set. Repeat with the remaining egg whites. Reserve and keep them warm.

5. To assemble the dish, place one tomato slice on the serving plate, top with a slice of Canadian bacon, poached egg white and a few tablespoons of the spinach mixture. Repeat for other servings. Serve immediately.

Texas-Style Meatloaf

Serves eight

Buttermilk and barbeque sauce give this meatloaf its tang. There are several tricks to creating a great meatloaf. First, do not over-mix as the texture will become too tough. Then test taste a small amount in a small skillet before cooking the whole thing. Remember to season heavily for outstanding flavor. You can bake this earlier in the day in the oven, and then place it on the stovetop grill (or outside grill) for a few minutes per side with a little extra coating of barbeque sauce. This creates a fine crispy coating.

INGREDIENTS:

>   4 egg whites
>   ¼ cup buttermilk
>   1 pound lean ground pork
>   1 pound lean ground beef or turkey
>   2 cups corn breadcrumbs (from freshly baked corn bread
>   recipe on page 60) or prepared corn breadcrumbs
>   1 medium Vidalia onion, minced
>   1½ cups plus 3 tablespoons prepared barbeque sauce
>   1 teaspoon dried oregano
>   2 teaspoons salt and 1 teaspoon pepper
>   ¼ cup pimento-stuffed green olives

STEPS:

1. Preheat oven to 350 degrees.

2. Whisk egg whites with the buttermilk and set aside.

3. Place the meat in a large bowl, add the breadcrumbs, pour over milk mixture, then add the chopped onion, one and a half cups barbeque sauce, oregano, and salt and pepper. Mix with your hands just until the ingredients are combined. Add olives and mix again, taking care not to overwork with your hands.

4. Remove a tablespoon or two of the meatloaf and cook it in a nonstick skillet over medium heat until cooked through—taste and adjust the seasonings if necessary.

Place meat mixture into a baking dish, shaping it into an oval shape. Bake for fifty minutes. Coat the top of the meatloaf with the remaining barbeque sauce and place under the broiler for three to five minutes until brown and bubbling. Serve immediately.

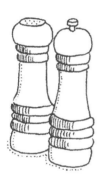

COOKING TIP

Make extra zucchini corn bread beforehand (recipe on page 60). Use some for the meatloaf mix and serve some alongside your meal with a great potato salad or coleslaw at your next barbeque, or as sandwiches the next day.

Sicilian-Style Stuffed Peppers

Serves four

These stuffed peppers offer a very satisfying meal on their own, with the combination of salty capers and olives and sweet raisins. If you use a variety of colored peppers, it is a beautiful and tasty dish to prepare for a special occasion.

INGREDIENTS:

4 large green, yellow, or red peppers, trimmed of stem and seeded
cooking spray
½ Vidalia (or yellow) onion, minced
1 pound ground turkey
2 tablespoons capers
3 tablespoons green olives, pitted and chopped
3 tablespoons raisins, coarsely chopped
2 tablespoons chopped parsley
4 egg whites
salt and pepper to taste
¼ cup low-fat ricotta cheese
2 tablespoons freshly grated Parmesan cheese
¼ cup shredded low-fat mozzarella or Monterey Jack cheese

FOR THE SAUCE:

4 roasted red or yellow peppers
3 cloves garlic, roasted
¼ cup chicken stock
salt and pepper to taste
½ bunch parsley, trimmed and chopped (for garnish)

STEPS:

1. Heat oven to 350 degrees.

2. In a large Dutch oven or saucepan, bring about four inches of water to the

boiling point, over medium-high heat Add peppers to boiling water and cook five minutes. Drain well and set aside.

3. Spray a large nonstick skillet with the cooking spray, add the onions, and sauté five to seven minutes over medium heat until they turn translucent. Add the ground turkey, capers, olives, raisins, parsley, and egg whites and cook, stirring constantly, about five to seven minutes. Season to taste with salt and freshly ground black pepper.

4. Combine the three cheeses in a small mixing bowl. Stuff each pepper with some of the turkey mixture and top each one with some of the cheese mixture. Place peppers upright in a nine- to ten-inch baking dish.

5. To make the sauce, in the bowl of a food processor or blender, combine the peppers, garlic, and chicken stock and process until smooth. Season to taste with salt and pepper. Pour this sauce around the peppers in the baking dish.

6. Cover with aluminum foil and bake twenty minutes, then remove cover and continue baking until cheese is melted and bubbling on top. Remove from oven, and garnish with fresh parsley, and serve immediately.

Perfect Crepes with Mushrooms and Goat Cheese

Serves four; makes sixteen to eighteen crepes

We both grew up being served plate-size flat "pancakes" by our mothers and grandmothers on special Sunday mornings. We waited patiently at the table for them to be served to us one by one and then would slather them in butter, lemon, and sugar. Now, we realize these aren't a pancake at all but a form of crepe. Here is our egg white version of the very versatile crepe that's great for any meal, depending what you choose to fill it with. For dinner use the mushroom filling below.

This recipe makes a lot, but the crepes can be stored in the refrigerator a day or two, as long as you wrap them well in plastic wrap. Then you can serve them at another meal with a different filling.

INGREDIENTS:

> 24 egg whites, equal to 3 cups egg whites
> 1 cup low-fat milk
> 1 cup flour
> ½ teaspoon salt

STEPS:

1. In a large mixing bowl, pour the egg whites and milk and whisk to combine. Add the flour and salt and whisk until the flour lumps disappear. Let batter rest for ten minutes.

2. Heat a ten-inch skillet over medium heat and spray thoroughly with butter-flavored cooking spray. Using a quarter-cup measure, pour in the crepe batter and swirl skillet to make an even layer. Cook one minute and flip over, then cook forty-five seconds to one minute more. Continue with the rest of the batter, spraying the skillet each time. Stir the batter occasionally as the flour will settle to the bottom.

MUSHROOM AND GOAT CHEESE FILLING:

1 teaspoon canola oil

1 small onion, minced

1 pound button mushrooms, washed, stemmed, and sliced

1 pound shitake mushrooms, washed, stemmed, and sliced

salt and freshly ground black pepper

¾ cup white wine or sherry

1 12-ounce can low-fat evaporated milk

2 ounces goat cheese, crumbled

½ bunch fresh parsley, chopped

STEPS:

1. In a large nonstick skillet, add the oil and sauté the onions three to five minutes over medium heat until they turn translucent. Add the mushrooms and stir, cook for five to seven minutes, season with salt and pepper. Add the white wine, turn the heat up to high, and allow the wine to reduce by three-quarters. Add the milk and goat cheese and cook another three to five minutes until thickened. Taste and adjust seasoning and add the parsley.

2. Evenly divide the filling between eight crepes and roll up. Place two crepes on each plate and serve immediately.

Should you really want to go eggy over your egg whites, you might try using portions of our Black and White Chili (page 110) as a crepe filling for lunch or dinner.

If you are serving the crepes for breakfast, you might try the classic butter, lemon, and sugar combination, or fill the crepes with your favorite marmalade, jam, or fresh fruit and yogurt.

For dessert, try sliced bananas and chocolate chips (or substitute chopped pecans for the chips, if you want to cut down on sugar). You might also sauté pears, peaches, apples, or other fresh fruit and mix with lightly sweetened non-fat sour cream.

Stir-Fried Rice with Egg Whites and Edamame

Serves four to six

This Asian-style rice dish can be made spicy or mild, depending on your taste, and will please the vegetarians in your life. On its own, this fried rice is a satisfying one-pot meal. However, if you serve this with the Asparagus and Egg White Nori Rolls (see page 94) and the Egg White Drop Soup (see page 72), it becomes a festive meal for a dinner party.

INGREDIENTS:

1 tablespoon canola oil

4 tablespoons scallions

1 bell pepper, stemmed, seeded, and diced

1 cup shredded carrots

1 tablespoon minced garlic

1 tablespoon minced ginger

2 egg whites, slightly beaten

¼ cup mirin (a Japanese sweet cooking wine) or sherry

2 tablespoons soy sauce

1 tablespoon sesame oil

1 tablespoon nam pla (Thai fish-based sauce condiment)

1 tablespoon hot pepper oil (or to taste)

3 to 4 cups cooked brown rice, cooled

1 cup edamame (cooked soybeans)

10 hard-cooked egg whites, diced

¼ cup cilantro, minced (optional)

STEPS:

1. In a nonstick wok or large skillet over high heat, over medium-high heat, add oil. Add scallions, peppers, and carrots, and cook five to eight minutes until lightly browned, stirring occasionally. Add garlic and ginger, then stir one to two minutes.

2. In a separate bowl, combine uncooked egg whites with the mirin, soy sauce, sesame oil, nam pla, and hot pepper oil.

3. Add cooked rice to skillet, breaking up the lumps with your spoon. Make a hole in the rice and pour the egg white mixture into rice and cook five to eight minutes, stirring occasionally.

4. Reduce heat to medium. Add the edamame and diced egg whites and stir to combine. Cover and cook three to four minutes to heat through.

5. Remove from the heat and transfer to a serving platter, sprinkle on the cilantro, and serve.

Chapter 10

Desserts

Love and eggs are best when they are fresh.
—Russian proverb

Ah, desserts, the bane of existence for the overeater, the perfect treat after a meal for the one who savors just enough and no more. They are a great way to show off and show your guests how much you care. We've used egg whites in cakes, parfaits, custards, and soufflés, paired them with fruits and berries, and brought the much loved meringue to center stage.

While these desserts do use sugar, we've suggested low-fat sour cream and cream cheese where possible. If you use a sugar substitute, you will have to check the sugar equivalency chart on the package in order to make sure you are using the right amount.

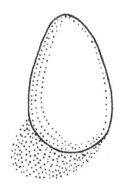

Spiced Chocolate Soufflé

Serves four

This can be made with or without the added spices and they will still taste divine, but the spices add a wonderful sense of whimsy and heighten the chocolate flavor.

You do need a straight-sided baking dish for this as it helps the soufflé rise up the sides; individual ramekins work great (see the soufflé guidelines for mixing, folding, and baking a soufflé on page 63).

INGREDIENTS:

cooking spray

7 tablespoons plus 1 teaspoon sugar

2 tablespoons plus 1 teaspoon unsweetened cocoa powder

½ cup 1% low-fat milk

2 whole star anise pods

1 cinnamon stick

1 ounce semi-sweet chocolate

4½ teaspoons unsalted butter

2 tablespoons all-purpose flour

⅛ teaspoon salt

3 egg whites

¼ teaspoon cream of tartar

pinch of salt

STEPS:

1. Preheat the oven to 375 degrees.

2. Coat four six-ounce ramekins with the cooking spray and dust each with a mixture of one teaspoon sugar and one teaspoon cocoa powder. Place them on a baking sheet.

3. Pour the milk into a small saucepan and add the star anise and cinnamon sticks. Bring to a boil and then cover the pan and turn off the heat. Let the milk steep for a half hour covered. Strain the milk through a fine sieve and return back to the saucepan.

4. Combine chocolate, butter, and three tablespoons of the sugar in a small microwavable bowl. Cook on high for thirty to forty seconds, or melt using a double boiler over simmering water. Add the melted chocolate to the milk in the saucepan, then add the cocoa, flour, and salt, stirring with a whisk until blended. Cook over medium heat for three to five minutes until the mixture thickens(it should coat the back of a wooden spoon), stirring constantly. Remove from the heat, pour into a large mixing bowl, and let cool.

5. In a large, clean mixing bowl, beat the egg whites with the cream of tartar and salt until foamy. Add the remaining sugar gradually, one tablespoon at a time, until stiff peaks form. With a spatula, fold a third of the eggs into the chocolate mixture. Add the remaining mixture in two portions, incorporating well after each addition but taking care not to deflate the mixture.

6. Spoon into the prepared ramekins and bake for twenty minutes. Serve immediately.

Banana Graham Pudding

Serves twelve

This retro-inspired dessert is best served in deep glass bowl to show it off in all its finery. Piled high with fluffy meringue, it hits the spot every time and is a real crowd-pleaser.

INGREDIENTS:

⅓ cup white flour
⅓ cup whole wheat flour
1 cup brown sugar
½ teaspoon salt
4 cups fat free milk
1 teaspoon vanilla extract
8 egg whites
¼ teaspoon cream of tartar
pinch of salt
6 tablespoons sugar
¼ teaspoon cinnamon
cooking spray
2 cups crushed low-fat graham crackers
6 bananas, sliced

STEPS:

1. Preheat oven to 325 degrees.

2. Combine the flour, sugar, and salt in a large saucepan and stir with a whisk. Gradually add the milk, stirring to dissolve any lumps.

3. Cook over medium heat twelve to fourteen minutes, stirring constantly, or until thick and bubbly. Add in vanilla extract and set aside.

4. In a large mixing bowl, beat four egg whites until frothy, add one cup of hot milk mixture to eggs, whisking to avoid cooking the whites. Pour this mixture through a strainer back into the milk mixture in the saucepan, then heat two to three minutes more, stirring constantly. Reserve. If doing this in advance, cover it directly with plastic wrap to prevent a skin from forming.

5. In large clean bowl, place four egg whites, cream of tartar, and pinch of salt. Beat with a hand mixer at high speed until eggs are foamy. Add sugar, a tablespoon at a time, and the cinnamon, beating until stiff peaks form. Reserve.

6. Spray a large three-quart ovenproof dish with cooking spray. Sprinkle a cup of graham cracker crumbs on the bottom of the dish, top with half of the banana slices. Pour half of the pudding mixture on top of the bananas. Repeat these layers and top with the meringue.

7. Bake for twenty minutes until lightly browned. Serve pudding warm or chilled.

Meringue Kisses

Makes thirty-six cookies

These delectable little melt-in-the-mouth cookies are so versatile that you should learn the recipe by heart. This is a basic recipe for perfect meringue kisses, but they can be flavored in many ways or colored with food colorings.

INGREDIENTS:

> 5 egg whites
> 1 teaspoon cream of tartar
> pinch of salt
> ½ cup plus 2 tablespoons confectionery sugar, sifted to remove lumps
> 1 tablespoon vanilla extract

STEPS:

1. Preheat the oven to 225 degrees and prepare two cookie sheets with parchment paper or Silpat (silicone) liners.

2. In a medium clean bowl, beat the egg whites (if using dried egg whites, follow the manufacturer's directions on the can) with the cream of tartar and salt until soft peaks form. Gradually add the sugar one tablespoon at a time until incorporated and stiff peaks form. Stir in the vanilla.

3. Drop by the tablespoonful onto the cookie sheets about one inch apart. Bake one-and-a-half to an-hour-and-three-quarter hours (depending on the humidity in the air that day) until dry but still soft inside. They will harden as they cool. Remove from the oven and let them cool on racks.

You might try covering the cookies in melted white chocolate, or using puréed strawberries, chocolate chips, cinnamon, coffee flavors, or food colorings mixed into the batter for different occasions.

Romance and Eggshells

During the Renaissance, it was an accepted practice for a gentleman to woo his lady by tossing a hollowed-out eggshell filled with exotic perfume at his love's feet so it would release the intoxicating scent when it shattered. A proposal at dessert time was the perfect setting for such an extravagance.

Rules for Making the Perfect Meringue

1) Start with a clean, grease-free glass or metal bowl

2) Use room temperature whites

3) Beat whites until frothy before adding any sugar

4) Add sugar slowly, one tablespoon at a time

5) Stop beating frequently and lift whites from the bottom of the bowl to ensure thorough beating

6) Beat sugar until dissolved, the peaks barely fold over, and whites do not slip from sides when bowl is tilted

7) Avoid making meringues on very humid days as it will result in a sticky, gummy texture

8) Use a low baking temperature for best results

Chocolate
Hazelnut Meringues

Makes two dozen cookies

These cookies are delicious and addictive, delightfully chewy inside and crunchy outside. We make them often for everything from fancy parties to school bake sales, or just to fill the cookie jar.

INGREDIENTS:

> 1 cup hazelnuts
> 1 cup plus 2 tablespoons confectionery sugar
> 3 tablespoons unsweetened cocoa powder
> ¼ teaspoon Chinese five-spice powder (or ground cinnamon)
> 3 egg whites
> ¼ teaspoon cream of tartar
> pinch of salt
> ½ cup white chocolate chips, melted

STEPS:

1. Preheat the oven to 350 degrees. Spread the hazelnuts out on a baking sheet and toast in the oven for ten minutes.

2. Remove the nuts from the oven and pour them into a clean kitchen towel spread out on the counter while they're still warm. Wrap the nuts up in the towel and rub them with your hands to remove the skins. Not all the skins will come off, but not to worry. Place the nuts in the bowl of a food processor, process until coarsely chopped, and set aside.

3. Sift together the sugar, cocoa powder, and five-spice powder. Prepare two baking sheets by covering them with parchment paper.

4. In a large clean mixing bowl, beat the egg whites with the cream of tartar and salt until foamy. Add the sugar mixture a tablespoon at a time until stiff peaks form. Fold in the flour mixture and chopped nuts.

5. Drop by the spoonful onto the baking sheets and place in the oven to bake for fifteen minutes. Remove and cool on a rack. When cool to the touch, pour a small amount of the melted white chocolate over cookies and allow it to set. Serve.

Tulip-Shaped Cookies

Makes fourteen to sixteen cookies

These cookies really do resemble tulips. While they are elegant and exotic, they are not at all daunting to make. In fact, they are a great way of showing off without having to work too hard. You will need at least one drinking glass, cup, or pudding mold overturned and one slightly larger in order to mold the cookies into tulip shapes. You may want to flavor them with orange, lemon, coffee, or almond extract instead of vanilla for variation.

INGREDIENTS:

> 1½ cups flour
> 1 cup sugar
> pinch of salt
> 3 tablespoons unsalted butter, melted
> 8 egg whites
> 1 teaspoon vanilla extract

STEPS:

1. Preheat the oven to 400 degrees.

2. Line a cookie sheet with a Silpat (silicone) baking liner if using, or butter and flour it generously.

3. In a large mixing bowl, combine the flour, sugar, and salt and stir with a whisk. Add the cooled, melted butter, egg whites, and vanilla extract and stir with a wooden spoon. The batter should be loose; add an additional egg white if mixture seems too dry.

4. Drop one to two tablespoons of the batter onto the prepared baking sheet with a metal spoon. Spread out the batter with the back of the spoon until you make a circle about five inches in diameter. The cookie should be about an eighth of an inch thick.

5. Place in the oven and bake for five minutes. Remove the cookies from the oven when they are light brown but still soft.

6. Have ready a drinking glass or pudding mold overturned and a slightly larger glass to place over them. Remove cookies from the cookie sheet immediately with an offset spatula and place on the overturned glass; press down gently with the other glass to form the tulip shape. Repeat with the remaining cookies on the sheet. If they become too brittle, you can place them back in the oven for thirty seconds to soften again. Repeat with remaining batter. Let cookies cool for about ten minutes before removing them from their forms.

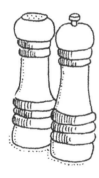

COOKING TIP

The cookies make ideal vessels for sorbets, ice creams, or puddings. Using a Silpat (silicone) liner on the baking sheet makes these infinitely easier to remove them from the hot pan. They require some quick actions when they're taken out of the oven so be sure to read this recipe through all the way and have your equipment ready. These cookies should be crisp—avoid making them on very humid days.

Brown Sugar and Ginger Pavlova

Serves eight to ten

This traditional Australian dessert, said to be created for the famous Russian ballerina, Anna Pavlova, gets a new twist here. Brown sugar and candied ginger pieces in the meringue give it a depth of flavor which seems just right when finished off with whipped cream and fresh fruit. This is a gorgeous, impressive dessert, a delight to look at, delicious to eat, but easy to make. For variation, sauté fresh pear or apple slices in butter, cinnamon, and sugar and serve this warmed over the Pavlova. Top with whipped cream.

INGREDIENTS:

> 4 egg whites
> ¼ teaspoon salt
> 1 teaspoon white vinegar
> 1 cup plus 2 tablespoons packed light brown sugar
> 1 teaspoon cornstarch
> 2 tablespoons candied ginger, minced
> 2 cups whipped cream
> 3 cups fresh fruit, sliced

STEPS:

1. Preheat oven to 350 degrees. Line a baking sheet with parchment paper.

2. Whip the egg whites with the salt until foamy, then add the vinegar. Start adding one cup of the sifted (no lumps) brown sugar, a tablespoon at a time, until the meringue holds stiff peaks. Sprinkle on the cornstarch and mix it again. Stir in the ginger.

3. Spread the meringue on the parchment in a large oval shape, smoothing out the top with the back of a large spoon.

4. Place in the oven for five minutes. Reduce heat to 250 degrees and bake for one hour until the meringue hardens but is still somewhat soft on the inside.

5. Remove from the oven and cool. Remove carefully from the parchment paper,

using a spatula and place on the serving platter, or carefully wrap the dessert in plastic and reserve for up to one day.

6. Prepare the fruit by combining it with two tablespoons of brown sugar. Spread the whipped cream over the top of the meringue and spoon the fruit and juices over that. Serve immediately.

CRYSTALLIZED FLOWERS

These edible, sugary flower petals make terrific garnishes on cakes and in special salads. They keep up to one year in an airtight container. Take fresh, pesticide-free petals like violets, pansies, or nasturtiums and coat them in pasteurized egg white, using a fine paint brush. Sprinkle them with superfine sugar and set aside to dry.

Chocolate–Chocolate Chip
Angel Food Cake

Serves eight to ten

This cake is our absolute favorite. It is so moist and chocolatey, it doesn't even need a frosting—just use a dusting of confectionery sugar on the top and everyone will ask for more. Although dried egg whites are perfect in desserts and power-health drinks, since your beaten whites will be cooked in this recipe, fresh egg whites can be used.

INGREDIENTS:

> 1 cup cake flour
> 1½ cups sugar, divided in two parts
> 3 tablespoons cocoa powder
> ¼ teaspoon ground cinnamon
> 12 egg whites
> 1 teaspoon cream of tartar
> pinch of salt
> 2 teaspoons vanilla extract
> 1 cup semi-sweet chocolate chips

FOR THE TOPPING:

> 3 tablespoons confectionery sugar
> ¼ teaspoon ground cinnamon mixed together

STEPS:

1. Preheat the oven to 350 degrees.

2. Sift the flour, half the sugar, cocoa powder, and cinnamon in a large mixing bowl.

3. In another mixing bowl, whip the egg whites (if using dried whites follow the manufacturer's directions on the can) with the cream of tartar and salt until foamy. Add the remaining sugar, a tablespoon at a time, until stiff peaks form. Stir in vanilla.

4. Sprinkle the flour mixture over the whites about a half cup at a time, lightly folding in each time, taking care not to deflate the whites.

5. Gently fold in the chocolate chips.

6. Pour the batter into an ungreased ten-inch tube pan. Smooth out the batter and bake fifty to fifty-five minutes until a cake tester inserted into the center of the cake comes out clean. Remove from the oven and cool by inverting the cake in the pan on a flat surface or by placing a long-necked bottle through the center tube allowing the cake pan to be raised off the countertop while cooling. After about an hour loosen the sides of the cake with a knife and release the cake.

7. Dust with the confectionery sugar and cinnamon, and serve.

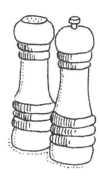

COOKING TIP

An angel food tube pan is required for this cake. It has a higher-center tube that elevates the cake when it is inverted and the cake is cooling, allowing the cake to keep its shape and not deflate. When the cake is cool, it has enough structure to stand up on its own. A special angel food slicing knife, which resembles a wide-toothed fork, can be used to make perfect slices or just use a long serrated knife.

Strawberry Rhubarb Pie

Serves eight

This is a classic chiffon pie recipe that our knitting group thoroughly enjoys. The pie is delicious and the ruby-red color reminds us of some of our favorite, rhubarb-colored yarns. Dried egg whites work really well here, so you don't have to worry about uncooked fresh egg whites not being pasteurized. If you do use fresh unpastuerized egg whites, you must heat them over simmering water and bring them to 140 degrees and hold them at that temperature for three-and-a-half minutes before beating.

For the crusts:

> 3 cups plain granola
> 1 teaspoon ground cinnamon
> 6 tablespoons unsalted butter or margarine, melted

For the filling:

> 2 cups diced rhubarb (frozen or fresh)
> 3 cups fresh strawberries, hulled
> 1 cup sugar
> 1 ounce unflavored gelatin
> 2 tablespoons freshly squeezed lemon juice
> ½ cup low-fat sour cream
> 4 teaspoons dried egg whites plus ¼ cup of water or 2 large fresh
>   egg whites
> pinch of salt
> pinch cream of tartar
> 8 large strawberries, sliced
> 1 sprig fresh thyme (optional), leaves removed
> 1 tablespoon brown sugar

STEPS:

1. Preheat the oven to 350 degrees.

2. Place the granola and cinnamon in the bowl of a food processor, and process until finely ground. With the motor still running pour in the melted butter and process just to combine.

3. Press this mixture into a twelve-inch springform pan, going up the sides slightly. Place in the oven and bake ten minutes until the crust browns. Remove from the oven and allow to cool.

4. Combine the rhubarb, strawberries, and half of the sugar in the bowl of a food processor and process for two minutes until smooth. You should have three cups of purée.

5. Take half of the purée and place in a heatproof bowl. Sprinkle with the gelatin and allow to soften for one minute. Bring two cups of water to a boil in a medium saucepan. Reduce the heat and place the bowl with the purée and gelatin over the simmering water and stir until the gelatin melts, about five minutes. Remove from the heat and stir in the rest of the purée, the lemon juice, and sour cream. Set aside.

6. In a medium clean bowl, beat the egg whites with the salt and cream of tartar until foamy, add the remaining half cup sugar gradually, one tablespoon at a time, and continue beating until stiff peaks form.

7. Fold the egg whites into the purée mixture one third at a time, taking care not to deflate the whites.

8. Pour this mixture into the prepared crust and refrigerate at least four hours. Mix the sliced strawberries with the sugar and the leaves of thyme and serve alongside the pie slices.

Pomegranate And Tapioca Parfaits

Serves six

These beautiful red-and-white-striped desserts are always a hit with family and friends. Pomegranates, although not too attractive on the outside, contain small red, jewel-like seeds inside. Our local green grocer sells just the seeds so it saves a lot of time, trouble and mess. If you can't find pomegranate juice in your local gourmet store or supermarket, and don't feel like juicing a pomegranate, try cranberry, apple, or grape juice. Use parfait glasses or stemmed water goblets to serve these because this dessert is so pretty.

FOR THE TAPIOCA LAYER:

> 3 egg whites
>
> 2 cups 1% low-fat milk
>
> 6 tablespoons sugar, divided into tablespoons
>
> 3 tablespoons instant tapioca
>
> 1 teaspoon vanilla extract

STEPS:

1. In a small bowl, beat one egg white until foamy. Continue beating, gradually adding half the sugar one tablespoon at a time. Set aside.

2. Place the milk, remaining egg whites, sugar, and tapioca in a medium pot, and let it sit for five minutes. Heat this mixture to boiling over medium heat. When it comes to a full boil, turn off the heat and immediately pour it into a large mixing bowl. Add vanilla.

3. Fold in the beaten egg white a third at a time. Allow this mixture to cool. It will thicken as it cools.

FOR THE FRUIT LAYER:

> 2 tablespoons sugar
>
> 1½ tablespoons instant tapioca
>
> pinch of salt

1 cup pomegranate juice or the juice from 2-3 large fresh
pomegranates

GARNISH:

1 cup pomegranate seeds
1 cup whipped cream

STEPS:

1. Mix all the ingredients for the fruit layer in a pot and let it sit for five minutes.
   Bring mixture to a boil over medium heat until it comes to a full boil, stirring
   constantly. Remove from heat and allow to cool.

TO ASSEMBLE THE DESSERT:

1. Divide the tapioca into two equal parts. Spoon one half of the tapioca pudding
   into the bottom of six individual parfait/dessert glasses.

2. Top with a layer of pomegranate pudding, spreading an equal amount among
   the six servings.

3. Top with the remaining tapioca pudding and serve immediately or refrigerate
   until ready to serve. To serve, garnish each with several tablespoons of the fresh
   pomegranate seeds and the whipped cream.

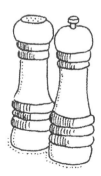

COOKING TIP

*To juice a pomegranate, slice in half and using a citrus reamer or
citrus juicer, extract the juice. Be careful; pomegranate juice stains
clothing.*

Chai Tea Pudding

Serves six

This large-curd tapioca pudding is brimming with chai tea spices and is ever so comforting and delicious, served warm or cold with sweetened ricotta cream or the whipped topping of your choice.

INGREDIENTS:

2½ cups low-fat milk

4 chai tea bags (or decaf)

½ cup large-pearl tapioca

¼ teaspoon salt

½ cup sugar

4 egg whites

½ teaspoon vanilla extract

1 cup non-fat ricotta cheese, blended with 3 tablespoons brown sugar

STEPS:

1. Bring the milk to a boil in a large saucepan, add the tea bags, remove from the heat, and cover. You will need to let this sit overnight in the refrigerator.

2. In a bowl, soak the tapioca in two cups of water. Place it in the refrigerator overnight.

3. After at least six hours, remove both the milk and tapioca from the refrigerator, remove the tea bags from the milk, and discard them. Drain the tapioca. Add the drained tapioca, salt, sugar, and egg whites to the milk in the saucepan and stir well.

4. Place over medium heat and stir until thickened, about twenty minutes, stirring constantly in order to avoid scorching the milk. The pearls should turn translucent. Remove from the heat and stir in the vanilla.

5. Pour into individual pudding dishes or a large serving bowl and serve warm or chilled. If chilling, remember to place plastic wrap directly on the surface to prevent a skin from forming. Garnish with several tablespoons of the sweetened ricotta cream.

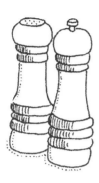

COOKING TIP

Whenever a dessert recipe calls for a whipped topping garnish, feel free to substitute non-fat ricotta cheese blended with sugar or sugar substitute, non-fat sour cream or yogurt blended with sugar or sugar substitute, or go whole hog and dollop on the sweetened whipped cream.

Five-Spiced Candied Almonds

Makes two and a half cups almonds

These make a great addition to any holiday buffet. Use them in salads, vegetable dishes, and as garnishes for desserts, or simply eat them out of hand. Your guests won't be able to stop nibbling. Use pecans or walnuts for variety.

INGREDIENTS:

> ¼ cup unsalted butter
>
> 2 egg whites
>
> ¼ teaspoon salt
>
> ½ cup sugar combined with 1 teaspoon Chinese five-spice powder
>
> 2 cups whole almonds

STEPS:

1. Preheat oven to 325 degrees.

2. Melt the butter in a ten- by thirteen-inch ovenproof dish and set aside.

3. Whip the egg whites in a medium bowl with salt until foamy. Add the sugar mixture one tablespoon at a time and continue beating until stiff peaks form. Fold in almonds.

4. Pour into baking dish and bake for thirty minutes, stirring occasionally until nuts turn golden brown. Remove from oven and let cool.

5. Store in airtight container.

Flaming Baked Alaska Cake

Serves eight to ten

This is a spectacular cake to bring to the table to celebrate a birthday or any special occasion. It's got its own flame, so no need for birthday candles. Use a rounded aluminum mold of one and a half quarts to pack the ice cream in and an eight-inch round plain yellow cake. Obviously, you will also need a flameproof serving platter, as your masterpiece will still be flaming as you bring it to the table.

INGREDIENTS:

> 1 quart vanilla ice cream, softened
> 1 eight-inch round pound or sponge cake
> 8 egg whites
> pinch of salt
> ¼ teaspoon cream of tartar
> 1 cup sugar
> 1 teaspoon vanilla extract
> ¼ cup brandy for flaming
> ½ empty eggshell

STEPS:

1. Spoon the softened ice cream into a 1.5-quart melon-shaped mold, eight-inch diameter, and place the cake on top. Wrap in plastic wrap and refreeze for at least two hours.

2. In a large clean mixing bowl, whip the egg whites with the salt and cream of tartar until soft peaks form. Gradually add the sugar one tablespoon at a time until stiff peaks form. Add the vanilla extract and set aside.

3. Heat the oven to 450 degrees.

4. Remove the ice cream mold from the freezer and allow to sit at room temperature for five minutes, then unmold onto flameproof platter. Spread the meringue all over the mold at least one inch thick. Place the empty egg shell at the top and fill with two tablespoons Cognac or brandy.

5. Place in oven for three to four minutes until the meringue gets nicely browned. In a small saucepan, heat the remaining brandy over high heat for two minutes. Bring the cake and the brandy to the table. Gather everyone around. Light a match to the brandy in the saucepan and pour over the top of the cake. Wait for the flame to extinguish itself, remove eggshell, and serve.

Impossible Coconut-Lime Pie

Serves eight

Also called the "miracle pie," the beauty of this dessert is its simplicity and magical transformation from ingredients blended in a food processor to an incredible pie that forms its own crust, custard, and crunchy topping as it bakes.

INGREDIENTS:

cooking spray

2 cups (1%) low-fat milk

1 cup shredded unsweetened coconut flakes (Goya brand, in the frozen food section)

¾ cup sugar

4 egg whites

3 tablespoons unsalted butter, melted

1½ tablespoons lime zest

1 teaspoon ground cardamom

¼ teaspoon salt

½ cup flour

¼ teaspoon baking powder

1 tablespoon vanilla extract

1 cup whipped cream (for garnish)

STEPS:

1. Preheat the oven to 350 degrees.

2. Spread the coconut flakes out onto a baking sheet and toast in the oven for ten minutes until lightly browned. Remove from oven and let cool slightly.

3. Place all of the ingredients, except the cooking spray and whipped cream, in the bowl of food processor or blender and blend for thirty seconds until well mixed. The texture will still be somewhat lumpy due to the coconut pieces.

4. Spray a ten-inch pie pan with the cooking spray. Pour the batter into the pie plate and place on a baking sheet. Bake sixty to seventy minutes until puffed and

golden. When cooked, a crust will have formed on the bottom, custard in the middle, and coconut on the top.

7. Serve warm or chilled with whipped cream.

Cherry Yogurt Meringue Sandwiches

Makes a dozen servings

These frozen treats are miles better than ice cream sandwiches. Kids and adults alike will adore them. Make them in advance, wrap them individually, and freeze. They will keep several weeks in the freezer. Feel free to stuff them with your favorite frozen concoction, ice cream, gelato, or fruit sorbets.

INGREDIENTS:

12 egg whites
½ teaspoon cream of tartar
¼ teaspoon salt
2 cups sugar
1 teaspoon vanilla extract
cooking spray
2 pints cherry-flavored non-fat frozen yogurt

STEPS:

1. Make the meringue sandwich layers. In a large clean mixing bowl, place the egg whites, cream of tartar, and salt, and beat until foamy. While still beating, add the sugar one tablespoon at a time until stiff peaks form. Add the vanilla extract and stir to combine.

2. Preheat oven to 250 degrees.

3. Line two large baking sheets with parchment paper and spray lightly with the cooking spray. Divide the meringue between the two baking sheets, spreading it out to a twelve- by sixteen-inch rectangle about three-quarters-of-an-inch thick.

4. Place the cookie sheets in the oven and bake for two hours until meringue becomes hard to the touch. Turn off the oven and let meringue remain in the oven for another hour.

5. Remove the meringue from the oven and carefully turn out onto a flat parchment-lined surface and remove the parchment paper from the top of the meringue. Reserve.

6. In a large mixing bowl, soften the frozen yogurt with an electric mixer by beating it a minute or two.

7. Place a meringue layer, flat side up, on a work surface and carefully spread the softened yogurt all around to the edges. Top with the remaining rectangle, flat side up, and press down gently.

8. Wrap the whole thing in parchment paper and then wrap in plastic and freeze for at least two hours. Remove from the freezer, remove the wrapping, and with a long slicing knife, cut twelve four-inch squares. Serve immediately or rewrap in parchment paper and plastic wrap individually and place back in the freezer.

Poached Peaches with Cream and Meringue

Serves six to eight

This simple preparation combines the best of ingredients: fresh peaches, raspberries, whipped cream, and crunchy meringue pieces. Delicious to eat and beautiful to serve, you will find this a good recipe to have at hand when guests are expected.

INGREDIENTS:

> 1 cup white wine
>
> 4 cups water
>
> 1 vanilla bean
>
> 1 2-inch-piece lemon peel
>
> 1¼ cups sugar
>
> 6 to 8 peeled whole fresh peaches (the peaches can be
>   slightly under-ripe)
>
> 2 cups whipped cream
>
> 1 cup crumbled meringue pieces, from Meringue Kisses (page 140)
>
> ½ cup fresh raspberries
>
> 12 fresh mint leaves

STEPS:

1. Put wine, water, vanilla bean, lemon peel, and sugar in a large saucepan. Bring to a boil over high heat, reduce heat, and simmer five minutes.

2. Add peaches and poach at a gentle simmer for eight minutes until soft. To keep peaches under the liquid, you can place a piece of cheesecloth directly over the fruit in the pan.

3. Remove peaches with a slotted spoon, cool, cut in half, and remove pit. Place the poaching syrup over high heat and bring it to a boil, and cook until it is reduced by one half. Reserve.

4. Strain and reserve sauce and peaches. In a medium bowl, combine the whipped cream with the meringue pieces and set aside.

5. Place two peach halves on a serving plate, drizzle sauce around it. Top with whipped cream, sprinkle with a few fresh raspberries, repeat with remaining peaches. Garnish with fresh mint leaves.

Long Live the Chicken and the Egg

Chickens and their eggs were mentioned in ancient Chinese documents as early as 1400 B.C.

Mango Sorbet

Makes four cups

This delightful summer treat is not too sweet and tastes just like the fruit. It gets its lovely creamy texture from the meringue. Try it topped with a sprinkling of shredded coconut and fresh mint. You might want to try this with other fruits that you love, such as strawberries, raspberries, peaches, or melons. You will need an ice cream maker for this. We use the kind that has a sleeve that freezes in the freezer and has a hand crank to process the frozen treat. This is a great job for kids.

INGREDIENTS:

> 1 pound mango pulp, fresh or frozen
> grated rind of one orange (zest)
> grated rind of one lemon (zest)
> ½ teaspoon lemon juice
> 4 egg whites
> ¼ teaspoon cream of tartar
> pinch of salt
> ⅓ cup confectionery sugar

STEPS:

1. Place mango pieces in a food processor fitted with a steel blade. Add zests and lemon juice and process until it becomes a fine purée, about five minutes or longer if mango pieces are frozen.

2. In a separate bowl, beat the egg whites with cream of tartar and salt until foamy, then add the sugar one tablespoon at a time until stiff peaks form. Combine beaten egg whites with the mango in a large bowl, taking care not to deflate the egg whites as you fold them in.

3. Place the mixture into the bowl of a one-quart ice cream maker and follow manufacturer's directions to freeze.

Jean's Spice Cake

Serves eight to ten

Barbara's neighbor brought this cake to her doorstep a few years ago at Christmas time. She remembers it fondly. Thinking the cake looked like a beautiful, snowy day with its quaint seven-minute frosting, we added a dusting of coconut flakes to this recipe to increase the snowy effect.

INGREDIENTS:

> cooking spray
> ½ cup unsalted butter
> 1 cup brown sugar, lightly packed
> 3 egg whites
> 2 cups flour
> 1 teaspoon baking powder
> 1 teaspoon baking soda
> 1 teaspoon salt
> 1 teaspoon cinnamon
> ¼ teaspoon ground cloves
> ¼ teaspoon nutmeg
> ¾ cup prune juice
> ¼ cup 1% low-fat milk
> 1 teaspoon vanilla extract
> 12 large pitted prunes, coarsely chopped

FOR THE FROSTING:

> 1 cup sugar
> ¼ teaspoon cream of tartar
> pinch of salt
> ⅓ cup water
> 2 egg whites
> 1 teaspoon vanilla extract
> ½ cup shredded sweetened coconut

STEPS:

1. Spray a Bundt pan with cooking spray. Preheat oven to 350 degrees.

2. In a large bowl, cream butter and sugar together with an electric hand mixer, until light and fluffy. Add the egg whites and mix to combine.

3. In a separate mixing bowl, sift together the dry ingredients.

4. In another bowl, mix together the liquid ingredients.

5. Add half of the dry ingredients to the butter/sugar mixture. Mix until combined. Add all the liquid ingredients, mix to combine. Add the remaining dry ingredient mixture and mix to combine. Stir in chopped prunes.

6. Spoon batter into prepared Bundt pan. Bake thirty-five to forty minutes until a tester inserted into the middle of the cake comes out clean. Place on a rack to cool.

7. Prepare the frosting: In the top of a double boiler, combine the sugar, cream of tartar, salt, water, and egg whites. Stir until frothy. When the water starts to boil, place top part on the double boiler and beat mixture with the mixer or by hand on high speed for seven minutes or until mixture is glossy and holds stiff peaks. Remove from heat and stir in the vanilla extract. Set aside.

8. When cake is cooled, remove from pan. Frost cake with the frosting and sprinkle shredded coconut on top if desired.

COOKING TIP

Seven-minute frosting requires a double boiler to prepare. This process is used to heat the unpasteurized egg whites and destroy any bacteria. If you use dried egg white powder in this frosting recipe, it is not necessary to use a double boiler.

Chapter 11
Misc-egg-laneous

The Simple Egg Yolk Facial

Both egg yolks and egg whites are tried-and-true ingredients for all natural facials. The yolks work very well for dry skin, while the whites work well for oily skin. Though both parts of the egg are generally good for all types of skin.

If you don't have the time for some of the more complicated facials we've suggested, you can just beat a few yolks while you are working on one of your egg white recipes and apply the mixture to your face, then and there in the kitchen. Then let the yolk set for ten minutes, washing off the mask when it's dried. The yolk tends to harden as it dries, and it takes a few splashes of warm water to loosen it. But don't worry, it does wash off quickly. This is a great treatment for dry skin. Think how beautiful and soft your skin will be if you give yourself an egg yolk facial just a few times a week when you are cooking with egg whites.

We find if we are scrambling up some Cheesy Egg Whites or making another simple egg white breakfast, it's as simple as egg white cooking to apply the beaten yolks to the skin and let set while cooking. Then you simply wash it off before serving and come to the table a bit more radiant and with the satisfaction of having given your skin a treat while also cooking breakfast.

INGREDIENTS:

    1 to 2 egg yolks
    2 to 3 drops of your favorite essential oil,
       such as lavender, lemon, or almond (optional)

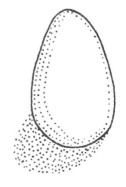

Egg Yolk and Honey Facial

When you've finished preparing appetizers for the evening cocktail party, this is a lovely facial to use while you take that essential time for yourself before getting ready to greet your guests. This particular facial is suitable for all skin types and you can also use it on your whole body. For a body treatment, just triple the ingredients to make enough to lather on your body, add a few drops of an essential oil, such as lavender, and apply from head to toe.

You may also give your hands and feet a special treatment. All you have to do is apply the mixture to your hands and feet, then wrap them in plastic wrap for about ten minutes, relax, and rinse off.

INGREDIENTS:

2 egg yolks
1 tablespoon honey
1 tablespoon vitamin E oil
1 tablespoon almond oil

Combine the ingredients and apply to face for ten minutes, relax, and rinse off.

Chocolate (Yum, Yum) Facial

This facial mask is recommended for normal skin. It's easy to prepare and good enough to eat!

INGREDIENTS:

   ⅓ cup cocoa powder
   3 tablespoons heavy cream
   2 egg yolks
   ⅓ cup honey
   3 tablespoons oatmeal, ground into a powder in a food processor

Combine above ingredients and smooth on your face or elbows or rough skin patches. Relax for ten minutes and rinse it off.

Egg White Honey Facial

This is a great moisturizing mask for dry skin, and a pleasant rejuvenating facial for any skin type. For all of the egg white facials, it is best to use whites from cracked eggs, rather than egg white product, they lend a better texture to the finished product.

INGREDIENTS:

   1½ tablespoons honey
   3 tablespoons plain yogurt
   1 egg white
   2 tablespoons glycerin
   ⅓ cup whole wheat flour

Combine all ingredients, except the flour. Then add the flour to make a thick paste. Apply the paste to your face and leave on for ten minutes or so. Rinse off.

Fruit Bowl Mask

This facial mask is meant for oily skin, but it is also rejuvenating to skin tone in general.

INGREDIENTS:

½ grapefruit, juiced
½ lemon, juiced
½ apple, cored
2 egg whites
25 seedless grapes
2 tablespoons chopped mint leaves

Combine ingredients in the bowl of a food processor or blender and blend for two minutes. Apply to face for ten minutes or so and rinse off.

Egg White Skin Toner

This is a great way to tighten pores and a simple way to leave your face feeling refreshed.

INGREDIENTS:

1 or 2 egg whites

Just apply the egg whites to your face for ten minutes or so and rinse off

Eggshell Photo Frames

You can use your eggshells to make mosaic picture frames. All you have to do is break up pieces of the clean leftover eggshells, use a white craft glue or Elmer's and apply it with a paint brush to your wooden photo frame. Apply the eggshell pieces with a tweezer to form a mosaic and press into the glue. Allow the glue to dry. Apply a craft paint with a brush or a water-based spray paint in your favorite color. Let dry and frame your favorite photo.

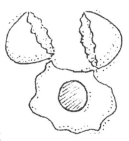

Egg Yolk Paint

In the middle ages, tempera paint was made by combining egg yolks and pigment. You can make your own today. Try this simple recipe and paint away. It is very durable and dries with a light sheen to its finish.

INGREDIENTS:

    1 egg yolk
    1½ tablespoons distilled water
    Pigment color, to your taste

Mix the yolk with the water in a small bowl. In another small bowl, combine the pigment with some water, stirring until smooth. Combine equal amounts of yolk and pigment until the desired texture is achieved. Use this to paint on wood or canvas.

Dying Eggs

To dye eggs naturally use Mother Nature's gifts and make a dye using very hot water and steep with the following until the desired color is reached. Use hard-cooked eggs. Place in dye bath until desired shade is produced.

- Fresh cut grass for green
- Red beets for a deep garnet
- Red onion skins for a bluish purple
- Tea bags or brown onion skins for brown

Throw your crushed eggshells into the compost heap to boost the nutrutional content of your soil.

Eggshell Seedlings

Another great use for all those eggshells you collect is to start your vegetable, herb, or flower seeds in the empty eggshells. Simply fill half of an empty eggshell in which you have poked a small drainage hole with potting soil and keep it upright in an egg carton. Water it and place on a sunny windowsill and watch it grow. When it comes time to plant them, gently crush the eggshell and place in the ground.

Peanut Butter and Oatmeal Dog Biscuits

Makes about forty-five biscuits

By now, if you've been trying these delicious breakfast recipes, you've either tossed a lot of yolks or saved them in your freezer, wondering what to use them for. Here is a perfect way to use up some of those yolks and share a delicious treat with the canine loved one in your family. They also make a great, unusual gift for the dog of the house when you go visiting.

INGREDIENTS:

- 4 raw egg yolks
- 2 tablespoons unsweetened peanut butter
- 2 tablespoons vegetable oil
- 1 cup whole wheat flour
- ¼ cup wheat germ
- ¼ cup rolled oats
- pinch of salt

STEPS:

1. Preheat oven to 350 degrees. Prepare two baking sheets by lining them with parchment paper or Silpat (silicone) liners.

2. In a medium mixing bowl, combine egg yolks with the peanut butter and vegetable oil and mix together.

3. In a separate bowl, sift together the flour, wheat germ, rolled oats, and salt. Add the liquid ingredients to the dry ingredients and mix to combine.

4. With a rolling pin, roll the dough out to a twelve- by fifteen-inch rectangle about a quarter-inch thick and using a two-inch dog bone-shaped biscuit cutter cut into shapes. Place these onto the parchment-lined cookie sheets and bake twenty-five minutes. Turn off the oven and let them remain in the oven an hour and a half until dried and hard. Store in an airtight container.

Conclusion

In the case of the egg, the (egg white part)
is truly greater than the whole.
—The Authors

Since our serendipitous encounter with our egg white lover at the outdoor market that spring, our understanding and appreciation of the egg white as a great, new, featured protein has come a long way with fun and delicious results.

We hope you enjoy these recipes and that you and your friends and family enjoy the fruits of your culinary laors as much as we've enjoyed creating the recipes and sharing them with you. Consider this not the end but just the begining of your delicious healthful journey along the Great (Egg) White Way. Here's to great cooking and eating.

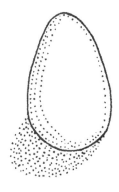

Notes and Personal Recipe Additions

INDEX